Many Moons

and a few stars

The First Part
by Leonard White

Edited by Simon Coward and Rob Moss.
Layout and design by Rob Moss (www.robmossdesign.co.uk).

Photographs are © Leonard White and their respective owners.
Text © 2010 Leonard White.

First published by Kaleidoscope Publishing, 2010.

Kaleidoscope Publishing
93 Old Park Road
Dudley
West Midlands
DY1 3NE
www.kaleidoscopepublishing.co.uk

ISBN 978-1-900203-35-7

The author

Leonard White's introduction to acting was entirely against his will. The whole idea of being on stage, performing for an audience, was an alarming prospect. He was a young schoolboy at the time.

However, most surprisingly, and remarkably, a particular experience changed all that and launched his long career, covering splendid work in drama in all media.

A wide variety of work with top artistes, walk-ons to leading roles, Reps to West End, at home and abroad, a rich career in a changing world covering several countries.

Now at the age of 93 he writes of his challenging fortunes. How Fate has seemingly created his life. And he hopes that his recollections express his enormous thanks to all those who have worked with him and allowed him such a unique experience.

Acknowledgements

Especially to thank my loving wife, Margaret, for putting up with me, all the time I spent away from my domestic duties, while up in the attic searching the archives and on my PC 'saving' my records.

And for my family, and son Stephen, and in memory of our elder son, Martin, alas such a great, great loss. And indeed all the White relations that I know, and I know not of…

I particularly acknowledge my good fortune in the learning I had from the Headmaster-superior, Ernest James Coker at Meeching School.

I acknowledge too, Leonard Crainford for supporting my endeavours at critical times, and Tony John for the important work at Coventry and later at ABC TV and, famously, Christopher Fry for providing the most important, challenging, watershed in my career.

Foreword

Trying to re-capture my ninety or so years of existence becomes a veritable "Everest" to relate. Thus, I can only tackle at first "Part One" of the long journey. Here I try to re-visit the first thirty years or thereabouts, from the mists of 1916 in the environment of the first World War, until the magic of the Festival of Britain in 1951.

From early growing up in the surety of Empire power, when the pound sterling was worth four dollars, when the pound was worth 240 pennies, and a quarter of a penny – a farthing – was common currency; until the shocks of the 1940s in another war, coming to our own backyards, and Lend-lease our salvation.

Amongst it all the seeds of my acting career being sown, and then the highlights of my works with the Stars. The American experience before the watershed…

I wonder if mine is a unique generation, moving from when wireless was a rare miracle and the moon but science-fiction to the god-like and devilish authority of today's inter-space?

Whatever, unlike Peter Ustinov's *Dear Me*, I do not write this for myself. I'd like to begin with "Dear Reader". And I hope that my story may engross pleasurably.

Chapter One

Curtain Up

It was half-way through the first World War.

I was born on November 5th 1916 at a house called *Brooklyn*, No. 73 Brighton Road in Newhaven, Sussex in a country called England. Not that I had any choice in that, and I'm not sure that my mother had any choice in that either. She was approaching her forties.

Many moons later I was told by one of my older sisters that my birth was in the evening brought on by my mother being frightened by a Lewes Rouser exploding. It was Guy Fawkes Night and the Lewes Rouser was the loudest firework banger produced especially for those archaic pyrotechnic celebrations being held in the county town a few miles up-river.

Perhaps if I'd had any choice in it I would have waited a few hours and made my entrance next morning, St Leonard's day. That would at least have made some sense of my being named Leonard. As it was I was dubbed Guy, appropriately enough, as my second category.

Not that I have any first-hand knowledge about that at all. Only a piece of paper called a Birth Certificate, and the fact that every year since then on Bonfire Night my birthday being marked, am I informed.

Strange isn't it, that we know nothing about our entrance into life nor have any control over it; and know nothing about our exit.

Certainly no one has ever returned to describe their death. Have they?

I was the fifth child of my mother and father, Maria Rebecca (Tasker) and Thomas George White. My only brother (also Thomas George) was eleven years older than me, and there were three sisters – Susan

Ann (for some unknown reason, called Nance), Eva Maud and Alice, all older still.

Coming so long after those four I think I must have been a 'mistake'.

If so, another 'mistake' came two years after me when my young sister, Edna Mary Jane, was born. So we were a family of six children; but more like two separate families.

Mary and I hardly related to the older four.

Alice, who would have been about 13 when I arrived seemed to have been given the job of 'little mother'; which I gathered later she didn't enjoy. Indeed I was told that on one occasion when I was being particularly cantankerous, she deliberately tipped me out of my pram on to the road.

Years later, whenever I'd behaved in some crazy way, that story was re-told as an excuse, to explain:

"What can you expect? He had that bang on the head you know."

If true, I believe I took advantage of that.

Brooklyn was an eight-room red-bricked bay-fronted semi-detached house, where I was born, built on the 'new' road to Brighton at the west end of the town.

Why it was given that name I'll never know. Surely nothing to do with New York City? But I wonder…? There was only one more pair of houses further up the hill; occupied by childhood friends, the Longly's and the Redmans.

Otherwise it was open countryside.

At the rear was a back-yard which had a shed that did duty for a hutch for our one-time pet chinchilla rabbit, and more usefully as a coal hole – storage for the fuel for the open fireplaces, the kitchen range and the scullery copper. The fire under the copper was usually lit once a week to do the clothes-washing and also to provide hot water for our baths. The bath was a galvanised-tin affair which normally hung on the wall outside the back-door and which was brought inside on bath-nights and placed in front of the fire in the kitchen-range, filled with buckets of hot water from the copper, and the ritual began. All pleasurable except for "soap in my eyes" – a large brick of soap, hair-washing!

When my sister Mary got old enough it was 'tub for two', saving water.

No indoor bathrooms or toilets of course.

Our lavatory was outside, at the back of the house.

Okay in the summer when I could leave the door open while sitting on the seat and watch the birds in the garden. But, winter visits to the 'loo' – often put off until the last moment – were fearsome, especially in the dark on a rainy night with a south-west gale blowing up my pants.

No lighting in this small abode, and so it was necessary to take a candle to illuminate those private moments.

Impossible to keep alight in the wind!

Nevertheless, when it was lit it enabled an opportunity to read.

No toilet-paper as such, but squares of torn-up newspapers hung up on a string on the wall. I usually searched for the pieces of the Sunday *News of the World*.

That paper was usually in the house, rescued from the left-overs, because Mother used to enter the Fashion Competition every week.

I used to take the opportunity in the loo to find those spicy bits for which that newspaper was noted, and which, for me, provided my private entertainment.

At the end of the back-yard there was a larger shed which was adapted into a pigeon loft. My father and older brother, Tom, kept racing pigeons.

There was great excitement on pigeon-racing days. Fancied birds which had been selected, were packed into their special wicker baskets and despatched by train to towns way up North, or for very long distance races, to release places in France.

Then, later on, eagerly awaiting their return to their home coop. Sometimes hours of tension, then excitement, the first sighting, then the circling above, and then the desperate whistling and calling to get the bird into the coop. A rush to remove the special racing ring from the bird's leg, and take it to the time-keepers to register Tom White's champion home. Hoping to win the Cup!

Beyond the end of the back wall in the yard, there was nothing but vegetable allotments as far as Church Hill and St Michael's Church.

A large area of well tended and jealously guarded vegetable patches, proudly providing healthy produce for the tables of many families in the Town. Well before the sanitised, tasteless superstores' fare.

'You've got to eat a peck of dirt before you peg out.'

Our allotment was a large plot that ran all along the west side of the house past the front door. Father had planted a long row of red rambling-roses along the house-side to separate the vegetables from the house. These made a great show, much admired by the townsfolk passing by.

Indeed many years later, when all the allotments gave way for a new housing estate and our plot became a new road, it became then inappropriately named *Rose Walk*, as the roses had gone.

But before that development, the whole open space, south to Church Hill, west to Union Hill (Meeching Down) and north to Bullens (Bollen's) Bush and beyond, was our playground.

"Cowboys and Indians" on the Hill, taking advantage of the trenches dug there to train soldiers for the real thing in Flanders. Ad-hoc football and cricket disorganised. Summertime cricket was notable in that our family and in-laws and friends did try to put together some matches, just for fun. And always a picnic.

"Birdnesting" in the thick bushes and hedgerows was a great attraction.

Competition was keen when egg-collecting was not frowned upon. But just the delight of bird-spotting was exciting. The hill seemed to ring out with birdsong; Larks and Linnets, Goldfinches and Yellowhammers, Thrushes, Song and the storm threatening Mistle. Raiding Sparrowhawks circling, hopefully not waiting for one of my brother Tom's homing pigeons… Dad kept a double-barrelled gun in the house.

I remember the joy of hearing my first Nightingale singing near the Highway.

Nearby, the hidden sand-pit was always a place of mystery. A bit scaring, the sunlight didn't get in there. I didn't hang about long in case there was something nasty.

Summertime was always glorious. I don't remember one not being so.

Blackberries and other wild fruits plentiful. Their harvest providing many a succulent pie home-cooked by Mum.

The excitement too of making my first kite (largely brown paper and string and a couple of pieces of stick) to fly the rising breezes from the South-west. Each flight a challenge to get higher and stay high; and then the magic of writing notes which would be sent up the string to the kite.

Considerably later, the kite turned into model aircraft. More sophisticated but not so adventurous somehow. The propeller, elastic-driven craft would usually crash-land on the first flight.

My long fascination with aircraft must have been seeded then.

Winter in the snow, the north-facing side of the hill was great for our sledges. Kite making changed to sledge building – a two-seater to take my young sister Mary on the back. If not that, then a tin tray "borrowed" from home would provide a mock-up and a fast ride headfirst top to bottom, and many a tumble.

Summertime contrast was soapbox downhill races on the new Brighton road. One powerless long ride from the top of the hill by the Golfhouse, right down to the bottom of the Town by the Bridge Hotel. An open road in those days.

All that on our backdoor-step. Free, freedom, fun and safe.

Oh, yes, and *Mary had a little lamb*. Among our many pets, sister Mary when young had a Southdown lamb which was kept on the hill near the chalkpit.

We had dogs. Three I remember. First a black and white Spaniel called Beau. He was meant to be a guard-dog, but on the occasion when we were burgled he enjoyed being fed a tinful of biscuits by the intruder, and never a whimper from him to wake us up.

Then came a large Greyhound, called Snipe. Dad thought he would race him on the Downs, but he (the dog) was too well fed. So was Dad come to think of it.

More dramatically, we had a Bull-Terrier. Whitish with a large brown patch over one eye. His name was Kafir. He thought it was his job to chase cats, and was very proud when he'd seen-off a moggie.

He really thought he'd achieved the blue-ribband when one day out for a walk with my father and me, he espied a cat and gave chase. The cat dodged round a corner. The dog gathered speed and followed out of sight.

Father shouted after him. The dog barked: not angrily but joyfully. Then silence. Soon the dog appeared again coming around the corner, walking proudly towards us, with tail raised (as high as a bull-terrier can). Shock-horror! The cat was in its jaws.

Lifeless it was dropped between my father's feet, Kafir's tail now wagging.

Total embarrassment.

Kafir didn't remain at our fireside very long.

I don't remember much about my very early days. Only two scaring incidents remain from the dark and distant. The first is of me in my father's arms screaming and trying to grab the gaslight in the days when the delicate gas mantle burned within a glass globe just above the mantle-piece over the fireplace in the kitchen. Apparently I'd been given some eel broth – my father's favourite – (he liked to go and catch the eels in the dykes around the river valley on the Eastside) and I had caught a small bone in my throat and become hysterical. I have a vision of fighting to clutch the light and my father struggling to control me. I have no idea of what the outcome was. But the visual remains – the moment frozen in time and faded like an old photograph. The nervous, frightening impact must have burnt itself on my brain, deeply.

Then later on my first encounter with threatening noise one night. I was scared greatly and had to be comforted by my brother Tom, who held me in his arms on the sofa in the living room, stopping my ears and eyes from the crashes and bangs and the flashes in the sky above.

Strangely I was placated by being told that it was "only gunfire" from the coastal guns on the Fort... not, as it really was, simply a very heavy thunderstorm. Odd that the noise of war was, seemingly, more acceptable than Nature's explosion.

Another significant photo-image burnt on to my very young memory was my first encounter with death.

My maternal grandfather, Matthew Carter-Tasker, had died in my mother's home village of Arlesey in Bedfordshire, at the home of my Uncle and Aunt, Arthur and Emily Webb on their farm.

I was taken there with my mother. On this occasion, one day I was in the house – the farmhouse, *Iona*. My vivid memory is of sitting upstairs in a front bedroom, beside the bed on which lay my dead grandfather. My photograph-clear memory is of everything being brilliantly white. Bright sunshine outside overhead. The white walls and low ceiling reflecting each to the other.

The pillows and sheets startlingly white.

The frozen face on the pillow, white.

The chair on which I sat, white.

The whole picture so white that no shadows existed.

I was sitting there so calmly. My memory has no emotion. The picture in my memory has me in it. It is not a memory of what I was looking at, but as though I was outside myself, seeing myself in the picture.

I have another early picture-memory, which also illustrates the very rural nature of our road in my childhood. The Newfield Hotel was next door but one from our house, and the landlord, Mr Winder was seriously ill. It was necessary for him to have quiet and be undisturbed, and I can still vividly see some 50 yards or more of the roadway outside the hotel strewn with straw, to deaden the sounds of the horses and carts as they passed by.

A scene of deep reverence. Even the walkers would tread quietly.

Is sight memory more powerful and lasting than emotional experience in a young life?

Next in my flimsy early picture memory photo album is an enormous, frightening pair of iron gates that seemed to me to extend so high above me that if I was left the other side of them I'd not ever return.

I was then four years old and being taken to my first school.

My mother – how she must have suffered too – was struggling, dragging me up the hill to where the large forbidding building stood.

It was the Convent where the Carmelite nuns, behind high walls, separated themselves and also ran a private school. Mostly for young girls, but they did allow young boys from the age of four until seven (or was it eight? Until they were beginning to develop anyway…)

I hated the whole idea. Mother was sure that she was giving me the best start. The reputation of the school was that it was a bit posh, and better than going to the Board (Council) school.

THAT certainly meant nothing to me. I was frightened stiff by all those funny ladies in strange costumes.

I struggled and objected as long as I could, but inside I had to go.

The gates closed behind me. Mother had gone.

Dark.

Of the three or four years there only a few odd memories remain.

An occasion when I was sat on a stool in the middle of a class of older girls to model for them to draw me. I didn't know what to make of that!

Embarrassing.

I think it was my first experience of any kind of religion when visits to the Chapel were part of the daily routine. I was not from a Roman Catholic family, but at that time I'm not sure that I knew the differences. It was an awesome introduction. And on other occasions we were made to dress in our Sunday best (the girls all in white) and process a long walk to a mock-up cave in the grounds to commemorate Lourdes. It was Corpus Christi.

On a lighter side the nuns always arranged impressive Fetes to raise funds. One in particular I well remember because I had a ticket in a raffle – my first gamble – and I won a splendid wrist-watch. I was absolutely overjoyed. My first "win". I don't know if I neglected to thank the right god or any god at all, but horror of horrors by the end of the day I'd lost that prize! I searched and searched but never found it. I didn't even get it home to show it off to the family – especially Dad.

Dark.

I don't have any memories of being taught anything at the Convent school. I do remember I never quite got to like the Sister Superior.

I was sure she had hairs on her upper lip.

But Sister Marie du Carmel was lovely. I fell for her. That made all the difference.

So all the minutes, the hours, the days, the weeks and months of my first years – and how each day was so long in anticipation in those young times – have added up to so few memories. I wonder? Can it be that everything is still there locked in my memory, but the right button on the keypad is not pressed to unlock those files?

The mother-board locked?

Life was about to change in 1924 (aged seven or eight)...

I went to the local Council school. The Meeching School for Boys.

Meeching (Myching) was the earlier 17th century name for the settlement, until Mother Nature throwing her weight about changed the course of the river Ouse and created a 'New' haven.

My 'New Haven' was now in this all boys environment. The girls were segregated in a school situated in the older part of town, between Christ Church and the Police Station. Protection all round.

At first, coming from the cloistered Convent atmosphere, I felt a bit different. I was nervy. I soon became a target for the heavy, bullyboy, Sparshott (I'll never forget his name).

But overall the lads made up a good cross-section of the town's youngsters and I soon found my gang: Osborne Hankinson, Arthur Duke (he went to South Africa), William Feist, Norman Elderkin, Leslie Clark (he was the one for the girls and made a fine Hamlet), George Lipscombe, and Percy Saunders (he was the footballer and went professional) – to name but a few. Helped too by my first teacher. There were two lady teachers, Miss Marks and Miss Currie who looked after the youngest. I was with Miss Marks. She was lovely.

She made up for my loss of Sister Marie.

Other teachers, the men, included two, Mr Cox and Mr Bulbeck who were the heavies, not to be crossed. Nicer memories evolved from Mr Hodges, who played the piano at assemblies, and taught chorus singing extramurally. I was never any good at that, but I made up the numbers when the school entered competitions held at the Corn Exchange in Lewes. I'm reminded of something similar when many moons later I found myself in the line-up as an extra on-stage in a film sequence in

The Courtneys of Curzon Street (British Lion), Anna Neagle was in the lead and her husband, Herbert Wilcox, was directing it. The scene was a big stage musical, all of it mimed to play-back, with me somewhere in the front line.

I'd never done it before. We'd never been told the actual words anyway, and to play safe I moved my lips as little as possible. My reticence did not please Mr Wilcox, who bawled at me. Not quite in the old way, through a megaphone, but it might just as well have been.

I lost my place close to Anna Neagle and got put at the end of the line.

I didn't like Mr Wilcox. It was the first and last time I did extra work.

But I liked Mr Hodges at Meeching School a lot. And later as I went through the standards, Mr Maguire, a fine gentleman, was my best teacher. Others included, Mr Burt, Mr Lapierre (he looked after the successful football team. He was nicknamed Biff because he was always shouting that to the boys in the matches when they got the ball).

I wasn't any good at Sport. Then there was Mr Marsden, and two student teachers, Mr Hersee and Mr Rae (He was the son of one of the crew of the famous Clipper, *Cutty Sark*).

Overall, although we probably didn't appreciate it then, our Headmaster was a brilliant man.

Ernest James Coker, in retrospect, was about 40 years ahead of his time, in relationship with education in the Council Schools at that time.

In the environment when everyone left school at 14 years old (some broke off earlier) to get to start work, of any sort, to earn money to help support the family, which was first priority, 'EJC' strove to encourage the boys to stay on at school beyond the accepted norm.

Class 'Standard 7' was the usual last before leaving, but Mr Coker created a 'Standard EX 7', which in effect was like setting up a Sixth Form environment, and for which he took responsibility himself.

And essentially the focus was on the Arts. Although I never remember it being called "Art".

During the normal class work, he would teach "Drawing" himself. And on one of those occasions I do well remember learning a very good lesson, which has stood me well ever since then.

It was fairly primitive pencil-drawing we were doing.

He came up to the back of my seat and looked over my shoulder at my effort on the paper on my desk. He pointed out – suggested – that a line was wrong. I immediately responded, sure that he must be right.

'Yes sir.'

And straight away I picked up my India rubber (eraser).

'Stop. What are you doing?'

'Going to rub out that line, sir.'

'Don't do that. Draw in the new line first. Then if it's right, only then rub out the old line. If you do rub out the old line first, you will more than likely just draw in the new line where the old one was.' How true.

Resonances of that piece of good advice have echoed over the years.

Beyond that, Headmaster Coker established and introduced Drama and essentially, Shakespeare, to his Council School boys.

Gently at first, with only 'scenes from' for the annual school play.

And that brings to mind a very strong memory.

I was picked to be in the school play. I hated the whole idea. I was enormously scared. I wouldn't do it…

I even got my Mother to write a note to Mr Coker, asking that I be excused as I was getting so het-up about it all.

I stood outside the Head's office door with that note in my hand, waiting to deliver it. I don't think it was particularly cold in the corridor, but I shivered. This was the age of the cane, remember.

Mr Coker had a strange involuntary habit. He would, especially when alone, utter peculiar sounds. At first a succession of quick spitting noises – not the guttural kind, but more like the tip of the tongue on the lips – and then added to that, louder "hmmm, hmmm, hmmm…"noises.

These together would start quietly, and then grow into a crescendo.

Quite unnerving, my legs shaking.

Until the noises would hit a high and stop abruptly

'Come in!'

Then I was inside, standing in front of that very big desk...

Why do they always seem so big?

Mr Coker was otherwise occupied and didn't look up. And then after a wait, spoke,

'Yes?'

'This sir...' and I offered the envelope across to him.

He looked up, fixed me in his eyes, and paused.

Then quickly took the envelope, tore it open and even quicker read my Mother's message. Without pause he folded it and taking it between thumb and forefinger dropped it into the wastepaper-basket at his side.

He looked up and again fixed me in his stare......

'Rehearsals start tomorrow, learn your lines. Now go back to your class, White.'

Dark. Dismayed. Distressed...

We were to do the sleep-walking scene from *Macbeth* and to make matters worse I was to play Lady Macbeth!

I would have done anything to get out of doing that. Even the thought of Acting at all, being on a stage, before an audience like that was horrifying to me.

From then on I was in a daze, and strangely and perversely I think that it may well have enhanced my 'sleep-walking' performance (certainly I didn't think I'd done more than get through the lines). But surprise, surprise I got a very good notice in the local paper!

Extraordinarily, and even more perversely, as it turned out, after having done everything in my power to get out of this experience; after being MADE to do it, to go through it, from then on I wanted to be an Actor.

In a wider context that experience in my education over 70 years ago makes for a telling comparison with today's philosophies.

Whereas today seemingly no child may be made to do anything the child does not want to do (especially if the parent takes the child's part and intervenes), it was the very opposite in my case, being made to go through a learning process abhorrent to me, and which had the very beneficial effect of releasing talents that I didn't know I had.

Headmaster Coker obviously saw something in me that I couldn't see and which when he had persevered opened up a new life for me.

During my last years at Meeching School – and I stayed on a further year beyond the leaving age – I continued, now with pleasure, to take up this new challenge of Acting.

I played several more roles, among them –

Queen Gertrude (*Hamlet*), Brutus (*Julius Caesar*), and on different occasions, Antonio and Portia (*The Merchant of Venice*):

'The quality of mercy is not strained…' and all that.

And notably Mr Coker decided to enter Shakespeare's *King Richard II* in the East Sussex Drama Festival (1935), which had the considerable attraction of having the final played in the Glyndebourne Opera House!

The various entries – there were fourteen Companies – were divided into two groups, each with its own Adjudicator. They were Arthur Ewart (Dramatic Coach and professional Actor), and Robert Newton (a Producer).

We had Mr Newton, who wasn't too complimentary about my performance as the Queen ('he appeared too het-up') and I wasn't too complimentary about him. But, of course, I'm sure he was right. I doubled up that role with that of the Lord Marshall, about which he was kinder:

'Good in voice and bearing.'

The local County newspaper gave a full page column to their review of encouragement to us, headlining with 'Fine performance by boy actors', then, 'Several of the actors were exceptionally brilliant. Special mention may be made of Len White who portrayed the difficult part of the Queen with dignity. A part that did not do justice to such a fine actor as he has proved…'

Even after that I was not confident about making it my profession.

I had not been impressed, when some time earlier our Head – entirely with the right intentions – had brought to the School a group of travelling players who were professionals, to present some Shakespeare scenes and (presumably) to 'show us how to do it'. They didn't inspire me and particularly I was shocked when visiting the classroom they were using as a dressing-room, after the show, that they seemed to me to be unwashed, and frankly, smelled horribly. Catching sight of underclothes lying on a chair that were obviously not clean, added to my repulsion.

I didn't want to be part of that. 'Rogues and Vagabonds'.

But, of course, years later I was to find out that they were not representative at all. Thankfully.

There was another boy in our *Richard II* production – Robert Embleton – who played the lead and was very good, and who was picked out by the Adjudicator, Robert Newton, saying:

'He was so good that he wished it had been one shade better and it would have been absolutely first class.' Praise indeed.

Embleton went on to Drama School in London and became a professional. I saw him at the Theatre Royal in Brighton when he was starting, but not long afterwards he got himself a "proper job"…

Overall, however, that particular production of *King Richard II* illustrated the remarkable work that Ernest James Coker, our Head at the Meeching School in Newhaven had achieved, and how fortunate we were to have been there at that time.

Fortunate for me in particular because that was my only conventional education. I failed the Eleven-plus so didn't get the advantage of attending the highly considered Lewes Grammar School.

The reputation of that school was confirmed for me many moons later when fortunately both our sons, Martin and Stephen, attended Lewes.

I must have been expected to pass that examination, because my Headmaster, Mr Coker, was shocked at my failure and contacted the Examiners to re-consider my marks. It didn't make any difference. But I knew that I failed before the results were announced. I was, at eleven years old, still a nervous lad. The exam took place at a school away from my home town and under the strained environment I just froze.

However, that school production of *King Richard II* insofar as Glyndebourne was concerned had echoes. As it turned out, many moons later, after I'd established myself on the Boards, I found myself being the Adjudicator on that famous stage for an amateur drama competition.

But back in the mid 1930's Headmaster Coker's created 'extension' class boys were beginning to leave school. He took the bold step to make provision to keep us together and continue. He acquired a large unused Chapel in the Town (The Primitive Methodist) to be run as a Boys' Club to house his Shakespeare Players, and he named it *Shakespeare Hall*.

A very successful venture while Mr Coker could continue. After that, much later, Shakespeare diminished, but the Club thrived still with some Drama involvement under training from actor, Bill Owen.

I had first known Bill as Bill Rowbotham. He had a bit part in the first production I played in at the Tavistock Repertory Company in London's Bloomsbury.

But I'm jumping ahead.

Early days at the family home and in the Town are now but faded photographic memories. Nevertheless they illustrate the startling changes over the eighty years or so. Radio in its infancy. My brother Tom putting together a 'cat's whisker' set.

Magic!

Then him building something more sophisticated, with valves, and a receiving wire aerial stretching the length of the back garden. And truly magical, getting up in the middle of the night to be able to hear the commentary of the boxing, Dempsey/Tunney World heavyweight fight all the way from America! The sound quality wasn't great but it seemed like a miracle.

Magic!

Those experiments took place in the room at 73 Brighton Road which was supposed to be the Dining Room. I don't remember it ever being used for dining. It was actually my father's office: a private place quite cut off from domesticity usually. It housed my father's desk. A place where nothing must be touched or altered. On it were a lot of good luck charms (He needed them). If he had a run of bad luck he – and only he

– would privately and carefully re-arrange them. Perhaps just turning a particular black cat to face another direction in the line-up.

I distinctly remember another fetish he had when on Sunday nights in a family gathering they would play cards. Stakes were small, but if he was on a losing run he would stand up from the table, twist his chair completely around, and then just sit down again.. Changing his luck, or so he thought. It became a family fetish.

My father was a Commission Agent. That sounded better than a Bookmaker, or a Bookie.

He lived on the nerves of daily Horse-racing. That untouchable desk of his, housed the important new piece of machinery, the telephone. It was Newhaven 54. The ring-up kind, speaking to the operator at the exchange in the town to make a call (there was very little privacy – the Operator became the source of all information and gossip...)..

Also, very much in evidence was the daily copy of *The Sporting Life* newspaper, duly opened to the *Runners and Riders* at the race meetings.

The 'Bible'.

A stock of tear-off paper pads and a small pile of his printed Betting Rules, together with newly sharpened pencils; all ready for those calls to be on the 2 o'clock at Newmarket or wherever; and all hopefully to be losers! When they were not, Dad's bad temper was rampant throughout the house. Mother usually got the worst of it.

I very nearly cut my teeth at that desk. As soon as my Father could take advantage of my ability to use the phone and write (and sound old enough. 'Speak nicely and CLEARLY') I'd be taking those bets over the phone.

They were quite educational. My arithmetic was sharpened up.

A "Shilling win" bet was straightforward enough – at least until the win was "odds-on", 10 to 11! Or, each-way maybe? Much more complicated when bets stipulated, "Up and Down", "Accumulator", "Any to come", a "Double" or "Treble"...and so on. I became quite good at figures.

Mother of course also took the bets when Father was out; but she didn't like it. She was only too aware of the riskiness of the whole biz. While she was working to save, he was losing it.

These phone bets were important insofar that they were legal, Credit betting.

These kept the right face on things; providing books and accounts for records. Ready-money betting was illegal.

His daily routine started in bed in the front best bedroom. Little or no movement on the Brighton Road outside, except perhaps a horse and cart or a flock of sheep being moved from the farm down the road to the pastures on the Downs. One of my very early memories is of one day when my Mother called me urgently to run and drive sheep off our front lawn, and get them out to join the rest of the flock going up the road.

Quite pastoral.

My father might not hear the squeak of the front gate as the paper-boy came, but would usually be stirred by Mother with his cup of tea (strong, it had to be strong.) and throwing his papers on to the bed. Then he would be wide awake to avidly study the contents of *The Sporting Life*.

Better not disturb him during that time, but I do remember a routine of mine, gingerly opening the bedroom door and poking my head inside.

I'd see that he was now reading the *Daily Express* and he would pat the bed beside him. I'd rush in and settle down for him to read to me the adventures of Rupert Bear – Mary Toutel's stories which continued for so long.

Later, I remember *Pip, Squeak and Wilfred* and I was a member of the 'Wilfredian League of Gugnuncs'!, but I don't remember the *Daily Mirror* being around very much... *Rupert* was the staple.

I graduated to the *Children's Newspaper* and *Modern Boy*.

Father would, arise when the streets were warm and the fires were lit, and settle down to anticipate Aintree or Plumpton; Ascot or Lewes, or wherever the horses were running.

Late morning he would spruce himself up – he always liked to look smart – and do his rounds. Always precise about his timing.

People in the Town used to say that they could tell the time by his movements every day.

He would make a circuit taking in specific hostelries, the Ship Hotel and the Bridge Hotel. The owners of the Bridge – Mr & Mrs Brewer (appropriately) became good family friends of ours. We children, Mary and I, used to love to have the opportunity of playing and going to many parties in that big ballroom they had in the hotel.

Big was big when young.

Then father would make a quick visit to our own shop which mother ran at 3 Bridge Street. It sold stationery, tobacco, fancy goods, and held the local franchise for Sunday newspapers (later it sold the dailies as well). There he would pick up the scribbled bets on bits of paper with the contribution wrapped inside. It rarely got to paper-money. More likely a "sixpence-each way" the favourite.

Afterwards on to the Conservative Club (he supported Admiral Beamish) maybe a quick game of billiards and finish up at the Newfield Hotel, close to home. Now with his "commissions" carefully about his person.

About 2pm a substantial dinner (lunch was not the word for that meal in those days) after checking the phone bets to assure himself that, at worst, he could carry the hot favourites.

And so to bed! Yes, a nap (no pun intended) in the afternoon was fairly usual. Sunday afternoons were only different insofar that after a heavy Sunday dinner both Father and Mother together went to bed "to sleep it off"…

Weekdays, he would be up and lively about tea time ('Pat, have you got my tea?') eager to see the Racing 'results'. After which he would either be as bad-tempered as imaginable and nothing would be right or he might break into a few lines of song, or even exchange a whistle or two with the tame goldfinch perched on the mantelpiece clock.

We had to be wary. I was often scared.

Never settled. His unpredictable moods kept me on edge.

In that room, his office, I was always attracted by the mantelpiece over the fireplace. An open coal-fire which, when not roaring away, provoked his bellowing voice shaking the walls:

'Pat! Put more coal on…!'

Why my Father called my Mother "Pat", I have no idea. He only used "Maria" on more gentle occasions. When he had time to relish the three syllables.

However. above the fireplace stood a rather attractive clock, in the form of a miniature long-case, and there perched on the top of that would be the free goldfinch.

Father loved this tame bird which he allowed to fly around the room.

'Shut that door!'

He had quite an interest in wildlife. Apart from the peripheral interest through his Bookie activity, he would attend race meetings around the country. Usually because he had a hot tip (he had a few contacts at Stables) and he needed to get the best odds.

Sometimes at meetings close to home, Brighton, Lewes, Plumpton, he'd take me with him. My main memory is of him pushing me through the turnstiles to avoid paying for me.

But a Bookie shouldn't be a Punter. My father didn't make a habit of it, but sufficient to stop him ever making much money.

In my earlier days, (and also before I arrived on the scene) he also owned a few race-horses. They were with trainers at Findon (T Young), Royston (A Day), Lewes (D Butcher) and latterly, at Bishopstone/ Tidemills (D Dale) where the horses used to exercise in the sea-water in Seaford Bay.

Occasionally, he would have a couple of horses in the stables at the back of the Newfield Hotel, close by our home. and there I had my first close-encounter with the Racehorse. Dad decided I should be introduced young; I think I was about four years old.

He lifted me up to sit on the back of one. The beast looked enormous. Not for long. I screamed blue-murder. I was off in seconds. It never happened again.

My older brother, Tom, then about 15 years old was much more compatible. I don't think that the horse owning phase lasted very much longer, and I can only remember one of the names – Golden Cup was at Findon with T Young.

I don't remember if any of them ever won!

When the stables at the Newfield Hotel became empty, my father put the great deal of straw leftover to good use. He decided to go in for smoking herrings (Where have all the bloaters gone?)

He would thread rows and rows of the fish on canes and hang up in the ceiling, then set light to the damp straw, and create a smoke chamber.

Bolt the stable doors and leave them to cook.

Result very tasteful bloaters, desired by all the family and friends in the private bar in the Hotel.

Delicious.

Other sporting activities that occupied my father when he wasn't dallying with the Sport of Kings, were, occasional duck shooting.

Dad took me only once on one of these shoots, at a pond near Blakeney Heights, and it scared me off for life. A couple of Mallard from time to time would make a change from the more usual Sunday lunch, roast beef.

All dutifully plucked and prepared by Mother, who seemed for ever to be preparing food, and which she did so well.

Also in the line of shooting Father was a member of one of the small-bore Rifle Clubs which held competitions in the range at the RNR Drill Hall in Bridge Street. He used to bring home his targets with the bull shattered to show how good he was.

But most of his activities were outdoors. He played Bowls in the Recreation Ground but notably was Captain of the team that played on its own Bowling Green at the Sheffield Hotel. Both those venues were quite a long walk from our home, and the set of bowls were heavy, and he would excuse himself from carrying them by insisting that if he did it would ruin his bowling arm. So either brother Tom or, often, I had to carry them.

He also tried his arm at running a field of Turkeys as a hobby a few times. I think not entirely successfully. But at least we were sure of Christmas dinners. It made a change from his usual Christmas ploy, when he would go into Brighton as late as possible on Christmas Eve and go to the butchers' markets in the Lanes and wait for the bargains when the birds would be sold off at closing time – that was BF of course, "Before Freezing".

I don't remember us ever being able to take advantage of Newhaven's "Turkey Town". That was the Eastside of the docks, where miraculously at Christmastime, lots of French birds used to fall by the wayside when being unloaded from the boats. The families on the Eastside were fortunate.

Apart from the early school influences in Drama I find very little in my family environment to suggest any ancestral background which might have lead to my eventual career in Drama.

My father did like to go to the Cinema. It was the days of continuous performance. Some afternoons when Racing was off, he'd go out and hail a bus just outside the front gate. Although the official stop was but a hundred yards or so away the bus drivers would pick him up at our house.

More like a taxis service. He'd go into Brighton and get off just outside the Regent Cinema to see whatever film was on. On return he rarely could tell us what film he'd seen, but he did rave about the Stars. The fact was that he slept through more pictures than he ever saw.

Much later on I remember him receiving a lovely photograph of Sophia Loren, addressed to him personally, which made him feel pretty special. That is, until he discovered that it was only part of some publicity stunt for a Sunday newspaper.

Deflation.

So, I hardly think any career influence on me stemmed from that cinema-going.

Neither, perhaps, was there when I started my own going to the pictures.

I was just about old enough to escort my young sister, Mary to the Kinema, locally. Mother wouldn't let us go in the cheap seats (four pence), so I was given one shilling (twelve old pennies), to buy two seats in the five-pennies and have one penny each left to buy sweets.

Henry Edwards and Chrissie White might well have been the stars (she, I fantasised, a relation, but hardly likely) in an adventure accompanied by our pianist, Mr Markwell, but the episode of the running serial, in the programme, *The Green Archer* scared me.

It was hands-over-the-eyes time; with a brave snatch of "between-the-fingers" peep now and then.

Although I couldn't resist the urge to see what happens next week, I had no feeling of catching the bug to be involved.

My earliest memory of some sort of introduction was the occasion when Mother took me and brother Tom to see a play at the old Grand Theatre in Brighton. I must have been about four years old.

I can only remember one incident. The scene was set in the booking hall cum waiting room of a railway station. Night-time and dimly lit. Cold with fog hanging about. I seemed to be in that scene, with my Mother, waiting for a train. I could see the ticket-clerk through the narrow grill where he sold tickets, arms akimbo with his head nodding off to sleep.

It was eerie, quiet. No one else about...

Then the start of a distant screech of an approaching train and building to a terrifying noise. I was frozen still in the booking hall; the clerk did not wake up... Until, with an enormous blast the front of the engine of the train burst through the back wall of the clerk's office and crashed through into the waiting room, where with blasts of steam it loomed and stopped, seeming to fill the stage.

Immediately the front of the engine blew open, and with more noise and steam, there outpoured from the bowels of the inferno a crowd of "little men" (probably dwarfs) all in green, like evil pixies, They swarmed everywhere.

From scared fixation on my Mother's lap in the stalls, I burst into life and turned and clung for safety around my Mother's neck.

I screamed and screamed loud and long, uncontrollably; and had to be taken out of the Theatre.

Not an attractive baptism in entertainment.

Another occasion was when my Father took me to the Hippodrome in Brighton to see Fred Karno's Circus. The memory of that was frightening too, because the acts featured ferocious wild animals.

Lions and Tigers behaving as threats to us in the audience. But tricks performed to amaze.

The Trainer daring to go into the cage with a wild Tiger, and then to leave the cage, have the cage with tiger inside raised into the air above the level of the stage, and surround it with curtains, crack his whip, remove the curtains and lo and behold the tiger had vanished.

Now that was magic! And my fright evaporated.

Now perhaps I could begin to see the attraction of theatricality?

Magic!

Playtime started to turn to play-acting at home.

We had a garage that was on the end of our vegetable patch near our back-garden gate. It didn't have a car in it for very long. And that car was something strange. I remember my father going to collect it from somewhere in Lewes or thereabouts. Dad took brother Tom with him to help and me for the ride in the "dickie" seat on the way back.

It was a green sporty French two-seater open-top.

It was a make called *Le Zebre*, A name I'd never heard of or saw again ever.

The ride back was embarrassing. My father insisted on driving home probably to show-off this new acquisition as he entered the town.

It made an enormous noise throughout the seven miles, and didn't let up at all. Roaring and burning oil smoke from the impressive exhaust.

Once home, my brother asked Dad why he hadn't changed gear?

No response.

He had driven the whole way in first gear!

The car wasn't in the garage long. I never had another ride.

And so, the empty garage became our "theatre". Young sister Mary did a lot of the organising in finding a table for the stage, some redundant curtains from indoors for the "tabs" (I think they were redundant). Sunlight through the open garage doors our only "floods". We'd write our own sketches. Usually poking fun at family and friends – and making sure that those same families and friends came to see the shows. I 'm sure we charged for entrance and programmes. No freebies, even for the loan of props. The audiences were often disappointing. Especially after they'd seen the show once.

Lesson One: Change the empty garage from "theatre" to selling our vegetables. More profitable.

There was just one other early theatre experience that certainly provided some influence. I was then in my mid-teens. I don't know what provoked it – except perhaps my previous school acting- but the father of my teenage girlfriend of that time (Joan Benger, she was) decided to take the two of us to see a play in the West-end in London. It was at the New Theatre, St Martin's Lane – truly the heart of Theatre-land – and the play was Chekov's *The Seagull*. Not perhaps exactly the stuff of teenage entertainment, but then maybe it wasn't meant to be?

Educational, I suspect.

But I was impressed. It was beautiful. Such good actors, the like of which I'd never seen, especially Peggy Ashcroft.

I think it was about that time I started to take the *Play Pictorial* and *Theatre World* magazines to keep up with all the 'real' theatre going on.

And it beckoned.

There just might have been some theatre lurking in my unknown ancestry: as was sometimes speculated. My mother's father – Daniel Tasker, or Daniel Carter-Tasker as differently called in various records, was a foundling. Anyway that's how my Mother described him during my young days; and alas, I never enquired or got to know further while she was alive. I'm very sorry.

Indeed there's a great hole in my research of my parents' lives before my time. Because I was a late-comer the greater part of my family were separated from me – grown-up – and my Father and Mother therefore more than normally ageing. I never knew much about their earlier lives.

I'm particularly sad that I do not know anything about their coming together. How, for example, did my mother – who lived in Bedfordshire – come to meet my father, who lived in Sussex? Their wedding photograph was taken in London! (John Hart of City Rd EC & Leytonstone Rd E.)

My mother's father is recorded as being the Landlord (Licensee) of the *Prince of Wales* pub in Arlesey, Bedfordshire in 1894. And by 1903 my father Thomas George White (aged 29) is named as that Licensee. So my parents must have been together some years before that. My older brother would have been born in 1905 and the three older sisters I guess back in the early 20th century or before?

I know that my parents had another pub in Trumpington (Cambridgeshire) – *The Green Man* – and a laundry in Old Southgate in North London. Once they had got together they moved about a lot: until eventually they settled in Newhaven, Sussex.

A large mixed unidentified ancestry.

Not a lot – if anything – to suggest Drama was in the blood.

Probably, father would have brought mother and the four young children (Nance, Eva, Alice and Tom) to Newhaven just before the start of the Great War (WWI). He coming back home, but mother and the family arriving for the first time.

I believe that one of Dad's sisters was running a sort of café (known as the *Eating House* in Bridge St., on the corner of Woolgar's Passage.) and my father returned to Newhaven to help her. Also he opened his own business at No 3 Bridge St as a wholesale newspaper agency.

Mother actually ran that business, and kept it going; assisted by my sister Eva most of the time. Sister Alice and brother Tom helped on and off…

Sister Nance, the eldest, left home to be a Nurse, during WW1…

Her boyfriend was killed at the end of that War, while on the way home after the Armistice. Later she married, Laurence Philcox from Brighton. They had no children. Eva married Edward Gasston, who was a Quarter-Master on the mailboats running between Newhaven and Dieppe. When I first knew him he was of the crew on the RMS Arundel. They also had no children.

Ted kept on the right side of his mother-in-law by bringing her goodies from France. We always knew when a "gift" had arrived by the particular smell that wafted through the house. Camembert cheese was her particular favourite, and she always liked to keep it in the open larder 'until it was really ripe'.

Alice married Lawrence Redvers Hibling, of Newhaven. I believe he worked for Harrods in London for some time, but I knew him as one of the Railway staff on the Quay dealing with the mailboats.

They had one boy, Barrymore, making me an Uncle for the first time, when I was still only a young schoolboy.

Odd.

My uncles were all old.

Barry married a girl in the town, Janice, and they had three children, two boys, Christopher and David, and a girl, Margaret.

Making me a great-uncle. And from that strain I believe that I'm a great-great-uncle: if not more removed. But that just stretches the line out of sight.

Tom, my brother, worked some time at the family shop: notably dealing with the Sunday newspaper franchise, responsible with my father for the early morning collections from the Paper train and distributing them to other retailers in the area. But then for a long time at the famous engineering company Alan West in Brighton. He liked rifle-shooting and billiards with his father, but especially his motor-bike, that is, until he had an accident, speeding on the Brighton road when it was little more than an open track. I think Mother stopped his "larking about" on that bike.

He married, Gwendolyn, a girl from Devon (Westward Ho!), who happened to be working as Ladies-maid at the big house *White Waltham* on Blakeney Heights where the Pizzey family lived. Mr Pizzey often did business with my father on the horses. He had an account using the convenience of the phone Newhaven 54, as many others did. Gracie Fields' brother (Mr Stansfield) in Peacehaven (where Gracie had her famous Children's Home) also was a notable caller with his commissions for the racing.

Tom and Gwen had one daughter, Jane. She married Patrick Attwater who was from Brighton. He became a successful Estate Agent and also worked for one of the Government Agencies. They lived some time in Telscombe Cliffs but for a long time in Folkestone.

They had two sons, Mark and Simon.

There were eleven years after brother Tom was born before I came along (1916). My mother was 39 years old. And then about two years later, Mary arrived .

I think that was enough for my Mother. I'm not sure that she wanted to start a family all over again after the first four.

But "family planning" was not much of an option in those days.

As soon as I was aware that Mary wasn't a boy, my memories recall 'taking care of her'. But she soon demonstrated that she could take care of herself. One of her very early 'sweethearts' was one of my pals, Monty Waight. He also lived in Brighton Road, but regarded as a bit up-market. He attended the only private school in the town – 'St Veronica's' in Fort Road. Whenever he and I got together to play games at our house, Mary would be keen to join us and make the rules. Monty didn't mind at all.

I, lamely, tried to keep things 'proper'.

Mary, eventually, married Ronald Trimbey. His family ran the Ship Hotel in Newhaven. He had been married before and had a grown-up son, and so was older than she. He was a fine professional cellist, and worked with several popular bands of the time as well as being a teacher. Later he and Mary ran several Public Houses, notably the *Hampden Arms* at South Heighton, and the *Rising Sun*, in Upper Beeding, and lastly one in Hove, *The Golden Cross*.

They had two girls, Peni and Julie.

The distaff side was dominant. Our male White line diminishing.

But back to my leaving basic schooling.

A leap in the dark.

Chapter Two

Stepping Out

Fifteen years old now – over three years beyond failing the eleven plus exam for Grammar School selection, and a year over the basic school-leaving age.

Mother was anxious that I got out from under the influence of my father's bookie business, to find a real job.

Leaving school for the real world was not such a wrench for me. For some years, I'd been loosely involved by having to help out at our newspaper shop. Usually being the paper-boy doing the rounds that others didn't want to do, like trudging along the old Brighton Highway delivering to those out-lying scattered houses and bungalows on the windy Harbour Heights, and the muddy Valley Road and Sheepfold Farm, in all weathers, and before school time. And of course I was cheap labour.

I particularly remember that on those occasions when troops were occupying the Fort on the cliff-top, I would lug a heavy paper-bag of the Sunday papers, on foot, from our shop in Bridge Street, in the centre of Town to the barrack-rooms on Castle Hill to supply the soldiers.

I had to make sure that I had the papers they wanted, and so carried more than necessary. Especially, the *News of the World* and the *Sunday Pictorial*… Spicy stories and saucy pictures.

Mother also trusted me to help her with the newspaper "accounts". Piles and piles of loose coins to be counted and sorted. Everything was for cash in those days. I don't remember ever seeing a cheque-book.

My personal "banking", such as it was, was with a Post Office Savings Account (sixpence in the pound Sterling interest!).

And I'd been used by my father in his Bookie business. That was much more exciting, but Mother was keen to nip that in the bud. She did not want me to get trapped.

She heard that a firm of Shipping Agents in the town needed a new Customs Entry Clerk. I don't remember that I ever had an interview. The qualifications, such as they were, called for someone "good at figures" and who could cope with getting up early in the mornings. Mother obviously sold me on both those counts. She knew I was good at Arithmetic and I'd had lots of training (against my natural will) in dealing with the early morning paper trade.

I was hired.

The firm was a branch of a French firm, Gondrand Freres (Courrier Express Gondrand), which had an office on the upper floor of a building in Woolgar's Passage in Newhaven.

Dickensian.

Gondrand's business was mainly to do with HM Customs clearance of fast trade goods entry through the port. Essentially women's fashion clothing.

Garments shown in Paris one day, would then be sent overnight via Dieppe, by Mail Boat to arrive at Newhaven early next morning. These goods had to be cleared through Customs and duty paid in time to catch the first mail-boat-train to London to be in Regent Street by the time the shops – Galeries Lafayette, one of their main clients – opened that same morning.

Grande vitesse – speed and accuracy was very necessary. My job was to calculate the Customs duty due, and it had to be correct. Any error – under assessment for example – could invoke a fine.

My experience with my father's betting calculations being accurate saved Gondrands some expense in that respect.

Otherwise I would not have stayed with that firm the years that I did.

The daily routine meant that I had to be at work at 4.30am to be ready to receive the documents from the mailboat.

These usually were collected earlier by one of our team, 'Bant' Bailey (why he was called 'Bant' I never knew) who would make a daily mad dash from dockside to our office.

There were about ten of us, 'clerks', as I remember. A very amiable crew. We had to be, to get on together at that unearthly hour in the mornings.

Our 'chief' was a Mr Blair, who naturally did not get to the office until the day had warmed up and his secretary, both arrived at a more humane hour.

Strangely there was another Mr White among us (Reg, but he was no relation); a Mr Robinson who helped me adjust to this unlikely set-up, and Stan Pope who had been at my school. I was the youngest.

Pope was a remarkable bloke for getting up early. He very often would walk some distance from his home off the High Street up to the top of the hill where I lived in Brighton Road to collect me and make sure that I had not overslept.

High summer, when the sun got up with me, those early mornings were quite lovely. Just me and birdsong and the occasional moggie off home to bed after a night's prowl.

I had my first sight of a badger one morning. He (it may have been a she) came out of a side street, ahead of me as I walked down our road. As he saw me, he tried to double his speed away, but his long claws – so good for digging worms – just wouldn't make contact with the flagstones of the pavements. However, he succeeded eventually in getting to the next side road and disappeared.

That was when to see a badger was rare, especially in a town. Now it is not unusual at all to see them in our back-garden at Hill Crest.

Domesticated, like the fox.

Winter early mornings were something different. If it wasn't plain cold it was usually rain and driven by a so-westerly. But the sturdy mailboat would not be late.

Getting up that early meant that after finishing work around lunchtime, an afternoon snooze was the norm. Nothing ever disturbed that except maybe when the occasional noise of an aircraft passed overhead. Then I'd be wide awake and I'd shoot out of bed to identify the craft.

It was usually a 'de Havilland something or other', or a 'Puss Moth'…

I was mad on aircraft.

A really wonderful occasion was when the *Daily Express* staged a glider flying exhibition on the Downs at Iford Hill, just a few miles away from us, up the Ouse Valley.

They had brought over from Germany and Austria two expert pilots – Herr Maggersuppe and Herr Kronfeld.

It gave me great excitement to be allowed to help tow-off and launch Herr Kronfeld's glider. And I saw Herr Maggersuppe take off in his sleek sailplane to make the then record long-distance flight – Iford Hill to somewhere near Southampton (or was it Portsmouth?).

The Master of Sempel, a great enthusiast, was running it all.

It took me until I was in my Eighties before I actually got to fly in a glider. Launched this time by mechanical means from a field near Ringmer. The pilot let me take over the controls for a few minutes.

Truly exhilarating!

But back in my teens, to first fly in a powered aeroplane, and that was with Sir Alan Cobham's *Flying Circus*.

A five-shilling flight from the fields between Newhaven and Seaford. Well worth many weeks' pocket money.

One of my early scrapbooks reveals other interests and some historic incidents, provoking me to keep the cuttings from the newspapers. Notably air exploits of that time:

'The Duchess of Bedford's airplane, Spider, *arriving at Croydon after her record flight to and from Capetown* [sic]*, a distance of nearly 19,000 miles. The feat was performed in just over twenty days.'*

The launch of the *'largest airship in the world – the R101 – October 12 1929 at Cardington, Bedfordshire'.* (That was just a few miles from where I spent many of my boyhood holidays on my Uncle Arthur's farm).

Subsequently, pictures of the maiden voyage flying over Nelson's Column in London.

And then, alas, but a year later the disaster, when the R101 came down in flames over Beauvais in France.

On a happier note, the cuttings of the spectacular and thrilling events of Britain winning outright the world air-speed Schneider Trophy races in competition with the Americans, the French, and the Italians. The involvement of such famous pilots as Flying Officers Waghorn, Atcherley: Flight Lieutenant D'Arcy Greig and Squadron Leader Orlebar, with their spectacular racing mono-seaplanes – the Vickers Supermarine Rolls-Royce S5, S6 and S6B.

So far as land speed records were concerned, I noted Signor Foresti's, failed attempt in his Djelmo car. (1927)

Parry Thomas getting killed at 170mph in his Babs car.

Major Seagrave in March 1929 took the record from the United States at a speed of 231.3624 mph, at Daytona Beach Florida.

American, Lee Bible in a Triplex car (owned by a Mr JM White – I kidded myself he might be a relative!) was killed trying to beat Seagrave's record.

Before that, the Triplex (three engines, 1,500 hp) driven by Day Keech won the record in 1928.

Another car, known as the *Black Hawk* driven by a young American, Frank Lockhart crashed into the sea at 200 mph at Daytona Beach.

But especially Captain Malcolm Campbell, who won the world's land-speed record twice for Britain with his famous *Blue Bird* car.

So much for a few of those early scrapbook cuttings. Exciting times post-war.

After leaving school (I'd become a Prefect for my last year, which I suppose was some sort of recognition?), I continued with Headmaster's Shakespeare Players at Mr Coker's new Shakespeare Hall: the old chapel building he had bought and converted into a theatre and club for us.

In 1934 we presented *Julius Caesar* in which I played Marcus Brutus:

'L White as Brutus was excellent and no praise can be too high for him, while his death scene, was superb' (*Seaford Chronicle*). A cast of some twenty-five.

Other ex-school players included S Tucknott as Caesar. The handsome Les Clark (all the girls were after him – if he wasn't after them!) played Mark Anthony, and notably, Robert Embleton, played Cassius. He went on to a professional Drama School in London. I saw him much later in a touring company at the Theatre Royal in Brighton, but he didn't stick with it. He changed for a "proper job" soon after that.

Other 'old boys' in that cast were:

M Robinson, H Bartholomew, B Matthews, H Mugridge, J Muttock, L Winter, L Harris, R Dennis (who played Portia), D Thompsett, J Vaughan, R Geering, L Giles, F Atherton, M Pope, D Boyle, J Pople, R Pratt, D Harvey, B MacGregor, C Haken, D Wells.

'Several of the boys were truly magnificent, and outstanding was Leonard White, whose interpretation of Marcus Brutus was in every sense a most finished performance' (*Sussex Express*).

Thank goodness I was now getting to play a male role!

After that EJ Coker produced *King Richard II* which was entered in an East Sussex Full-length Drama Festival (November 1935) and was Adjudicated by Producer, Robert Newton, as I reported earlier.

I was back (UGH!) playing the Queen to King Richard. Mr Coker was, I'm sure, presenting an 'all male' company as it would have been originally, and hoping for a few bonus marks from the judge, which he got.

'He wished especially to congratulate the producer. Mr EJ Coker, who had much to be complimented on.' (Applause.)

Fortunately I was able to double-up with a male role, playing, also, the Lord Marshall. For which, many thanks.

The rest of Mr Coker's players remained almost all the same as before; Les Clark as Henry Bolingbroke was again the nearest we had to a matinee idol in the gang.

But two new names appeared, E Hall and J Postles.

I have to mention all these names. I doubt whether any of them have ever written their own memoirs, and this will at least keep them alive, I trust.

My efforts with the female role did fortunately get some recognition from the critic in the *Sussex Express* (November 22, 1935):

'special mention may be made of Len White, who portrayed the difficult part of the Queen with dignity. It was a part that did not do justice to such a fine actor as he has proved in the past'.

The final of this Festival was held at the original Glyndebourne Opera House. We did not make it to the stage there, but enjoyed being in the audience. It was a fine occasion.

A great contribution by John Christie, who had created that lovely opera house in our Sussex countryside.

That was in the days of the East Sussex Rural Community Council; an organisation greatly missed today.

My working hours in the early teens were not ideal for social life, but I did have a few girl friends on and off.

Jean Bateup, Joan Benger, Anita Horlock among them, but I was beginning to focus on getting away to London to try to get some professional training

Only one, Joan Stringer, was different and remained a friend for so many years.

She was the youngest daughter of a family of girls.

Her father had come from the North to set-up the first electricity power-station in Newhaven.

The days when even small towns were as good as 'self-contained', self-sufficient; and the better for it.

One of Joan's elder sisters, Dora, married in the town, to seaman, George Bailey, and stayed behind when Joan had to move with her parents back North – to the Stockport area, and afterwards to Scotland.

I was, however, able to keep in touch with Joan through her sister, Dora, locally, and eventually Joan married to Garden West and settled to stay in Scotland and raise her lovely family.

We kept in touch, happily.

But with me, when a teenager, I was still scanning possibilities to advance my attempts to be an Actor.

I saw an advert – I think it was in *The Stage* – for film auditions, at an address in Wardour Street London.

There was a fee – which ought to have warned me right away, but of course I was too naïve. My father did warn me, but I was not to be put off. Reluctantly he decided to attend with me, and off to Soho we went.

I had been informed to prepare a "short piece" for the test, and I could only think of doing Shakespeare's 'The quality of mercy…' speech! Anything more inappropriate could not be imagined! But, I was on my way…

The "studio" turned out to be lower ground floor beneath an old office block, a bare room, and the only equipment was a microphone on a stand.

There was no queue stampeding to get in.

Just the barest of formalities, and I was doing my speech.

I wasn't asked to do it again.

I never found out if there were any cameras? I didn't see any studio lights.

In a few minutes I was given a copy of a metal disc on which had been recorded (very poorly) my recitation – for that was all it was – to keep. (I've still got it somewhere!)

Sharply, Father had whisked me off back to Victoria Station and home. Kindly he did not ring out "I told you so".

His Bookie training over the years had provided plenty of experience of losers.

I put it down to experience, and waited.

Later I discovered that the Royal Academy of Dramatic Art provided one free scholarship for a boy and another for a girl – The Leverhulme Scholarship.

Now that was more like it, at the heart of professional training for the 'biz'.

I applied.

What a difference from the former experience!

A real thrill to enter the building on Gower Street and feel the excitement of those serious young pretenders.

It was so good to stand on that stage in proper lighting to 'give' my audition pieces to the judges, somewhere out there in the dark. This time the pieces were chosen for me, and so more challenging (I can't remember what they were).

Afterwards it was a matter of waiting days – it seemed more like weeks – to get a result.

I daren't hope. All the other competitors were so good.

Surprise, surprise, I did get a re-call!

I couldn't believe my good fortune. But now was the toughest test.

It was, between me and only a few others – four or five I think?

Alas, I didn't make it.

There was a suggestion that I might get a part-grant, but I couldn't consider that. At least I was acceptable, but not for that scholarship.

However, the fact that I had gone to the 'final' for the Leverhulme scholarship gave me considerable confidence.

I wouldn't give up now.

My next step was to plan to move to find some work in London.

I had a cousin living in Finsbury Park (Jessie Edwards nee Ellis, daughter of one of Dad's sisters, Aunt Maria), who I had known quite well when she had been living in Newhaven. She, with her husband Ernie had been running a tailor's shop in the High Street.

They had indicated that if ever I did get a job in London I could lodge with them.

And I did get a job in the City.

Fortunately more or less the same as I'd been doing at Gondrands – Customs Entry Clerk – in Newhaven.

But here the difference was that the trade was with Germany, largely through the port of Harwich.

Blessedly in London the hours were more human, being 9 to 6.

The firm was CWJ Miller with offices in Salisbury House, London Wall. A not large, all male staff, occasionally enlivened considerably by visits from Mr Miller's, daughter, Jean. Mr Miller had a partner, a Mr Jacob who appeared from his office from time to time and dashed back out of sight as soon as he could.

I never heard him speak much, and never English.

I often have wondered since what might have happened to him when the war broke out? I hope all was well.

I enjoyed working there.

I might have fancied my chances with the boss's daughter but I was soon to meet my true love. I didn't know it then but she was working in that same office building.

I made a particular pal in a fellow clerk in this new job. He was Eldred Burrows. A first name I'd never heard of before, and I don't think I have ever since. We called him Mick.

Those were the days when mid-morning coffee breaks were allowed and Burrows and I used to daily – like very many others from Salisbury House – go across the road to the Lyons tea-shop in London Wall for our refreshment.

Those were the days when those excellent teashops in the City catered for more than just the vitals.

It was part of the service to indulge in a game (cards, chess, draughts etc) if wanted. The environment was more like a club, with the daily customers the 'members'. The staff knew everyone by name.

Burrows and I were regulars. Same time each day, and same table, same 'Nippie', waitress.

That Lyons teashop later on provided a great turning point in my life.

But now settling in London I was trying to see as much theatre as I could. My scrap-book reminds me that I was also quite keen on sketching. I was very impressed by the performances of Jean Forbes-Robertson, Barbara Everest and Raymond Huntley in JB Priestley's *Time and the Conways* (one of his *Time* plays), provoking me to sketch those three actors and send my efforts to the Manager at the Duchess Theatre (James Davis).

His reply (November 30, 1937) requested my 'permission to retain them until Mr Priestley returns from America. In the meantime we are showing them to the artists concerned as we know they will be delighted.'

At least I didn't get them sent back …

It was about this time that I had a stroke of good fortune, under unlikely circumstances.

I had a spell in Hackney Hospital (Homerton High St) with appendicitis. Workmate, Mick Burrows came to visit me and, immediately on arrival at my bedside, fainted!

Consternation!

Nurses had to turn their attention to him rather than to me.

However, when revived, he revealed that he had brought me a copy of a theatre magazine which might interest me.

That was a happy accident, because in that magazine I read of a company called Tavistock Repertory Company and the 'Tavistock' didn't refer to the town in Devon, but to Tavistock Place in Bloomsbury.

This looked very attractive, and as soon as I was out of that hospital bed, I got in touch with them.

Their theatre was a part of an institution called the Mary Ward Settlement, and was presenting very high standard work. That Spring programme listed:

The Race with the Shadow (Wilhelm von Scholz – Trans: Graham & Tristan Rawson) – A first public West-end performance.

The Sea-gull (Anton Chekov).

Major Barbara (Bernard Shaw).

Judgment Day (Elmer Rice).

The Anatomist (James Bridie).

Mesmer (Beverley Nichols) – First London Production.

An impressive and challenging season attracting a large company, including pro-actors 'resting' and wanting to be part of their programme.

A good stimulating pro-am mix and environment.

I was eager.

I was asked to attend a reading of the Elmer Rice play *Judgment Day* – aptly named for me – which needed some walk-ons. (They even auditioned walk-ons!)

Much to my surprise I was upgraded.

I came away having been given by the Producer, Leonard Crainford, a small part, Dr Mensch.

I was in.

There were 46 in that cast, including 'pros' like William Rowbotham (later known as Bill Owen), John Blain, Leonard Pearce, Jack Wing, Malcolm Hayes, Margaret Godwin, Jack Newmark, Kay Gardner, Jane Kaye, Lionel Hamilton, Peggy Watson, Neil Wilson…

That production opened on February 25th 1938.

That year marked another special event, indeed the very special turning point in my life.

At work, I was still going through the daily routines, still with mate Burrows taking our elevenses across the road in 'our' London Wall, Lyons teashop. But there was a particular difference.

Each day while taking our usual table, I had become very interested in another table, at which, also regularly, sat two young ladies. Well, I was particularly interested in one of them…

More than interested.

She was an enormously attractive young girl.

For a while it was a matter of admiring from across the room, but with intent to try to find an excuse to get to sit at that other table.

Eventually, without any excuse, I couldn't bear it any longer, and even while there were other tables clearly available, we made the approach direct!

Burrows said it: 'Do you mind if we sit here?'

Glory-be, they didn't mind.

I have no idea of how the conversation went on from that moment, or even if there was much or little or any.

All I know is that it was a moment such as I'd never felt before. And, I mean, felt.

Prior to that if I'd been asked about "love at first sight" I'd have shrugged-off the whole idea as nonsense, but this must surely be it.

Doubtless!

We discovered their names were, Margaret and Sadie, but it was Margaret only I had seen.

She was 17.

Thankfully, they both worked, as we did, across the road in Salisbury House, but they in a firm of Stockbrokers, Morrison & Morrison.

It was June 17th 1938 at about 11am.

'Red Rose Day', as it became and still is.

We are still celebrating that, nearly seventy years later.

But back in the 'thirties, we added lunchtime to coffee-time; and gradually got to know each other.

In the City in those days, some of the churches would regularly hold short services and concerts for the office workers at lunchtimes. We often used to attend St Stephens in Coleman Street together.

And as time past Margaret would also make theatre visits with me in the West-end.

Those were the days when it was usual to get to the theatre early and for a small payment put down a stool in a queue to secure a place to buy a ticket for the gallery or pit when the doors opened.

I liked the pit. It wasn't so far from the stalls as the gods.

The queue entertainers were good too.

All sorts; singers, musicians, jugglers, acrobats...

But one of those acts lingers with pleasure.

A sort-of "Wilson, Keppel and Betty" act, each dressed in something like a striped nightshirt, a fez and sandals. They used to sprinkle a little sand on the ground, and proceed to dance a soft-shoe-shuffle to music of *In a Persian market...*

They always went down very well with the queue, and raised a few bob. Always assuring a good start to the show.

I loved it.

During that period my old theatre programmes record that over sixty visits to London's theatres were made! Obviously catching up with as much as I could before the curtain came down, as it did eventually.

Margaret was Margaret Winifred Kent. She had been born in Wimbledon, but at that time was living with her Mum and Dad and much younger brother Roger, in Hounslow East. The new estate there, close to the Heath, was reckoned to be healthier then the part of Wimbledon where she had lived.

She daily had the long Underground train journey up to the City, in the days when cheap-day tickets were available if you bought a "Workman's" before 7am.

The Piccadilly Line became our connection, with me being at Finsbury Park and Margaret at Hounslow-East. A long journey but always worth it.

At weekends that summer it was often my route, to join her and make our regular walks along the Thames banks around Isleworth, Syon House and about.

Walks that often would be just strolling without a word between us. Eventually, I took whatever opportunity I could to "pose the question", but the question had no response.

It wasn't 'no', fortunately, so I never gave up.

Actually, Margaret was not liking the idea of me being an Actor as a career. She went along with my theatre activity as far as it went, and helped me, but was not so sure when contemplating the 'resting' elements of the undependable career I was anticipating.

I was torn, but the smell of the greasepaint was strong.

After *Judgment Day* at the Tavistock Little Theatre, I had the opportunity to join a Group Theatre production under the Producer, Rupert Doone. It was a new play by Stephen Spender, *Trial of a Judge*. A professional production, but which needed four 'students' to join and make up a group of communist prisoners, to provide chorus verse speaking.

I was one of those. It was in effect the first time I played in a proper professional company. I learnt a lot.

The lead was played by Godfrey Kenton and others in the cast were, Peter Copley, Aidan Turner, Colin Eaton, Constance Foljambe, Moran Caplat, Julian Somers, Emma Trechman, Kenneth Evans, Kathleen Boutall, Evan John, Peter Bennett, Bill Sykes, and in my verse-speaking group were, Neil Gibson, George Windred, Richard Wordsworth, H Dagnall, JW Maule, F Spelling...

The scenery was designed and painted by John Piper.

The stage Manager was Ian Atkins.

So many names that resonate through the years.

The production by Group Theatre was presented (May 1938) at the Unity Theatre, which had such a strong reputation in the Thirties.

I was back with the Tavistock Rep during their summer season, playing in Denis Johnston's *The Moon in the Yellow River*, Produced by Frank OM Smith.

I was playing Commandant Lanigan.

Also in that cast were, Jane Kaye, Jack Richman,

Alan Hood, John Blain, Henry F Wilkins... (May 1938)

The Tavistock also took a production on tour to South Wales during the summers, and this the second year, we toured Andre Obey's *Noah* in which I disappeared into the skin of The Lion.

The Ark was first seen at our London theatre on July 5 1938 and set sail to open in Trealaw (across the valley from Tonypandy) on July 11th. Then to Bargoed, Pontypool, Pontypridd and Risca.

Mostly one-night stands. Playing to packed houses of enthusiastic audiences.

'probably the most brilliant acting ever seen in Pontypridd...will live in many memories...and easy to prophesy that many will be turned away when next the Company come to the town...an exceptional performance' (*Pontypridd Observer*).

A great experience fitting me up (pun intended!) for similar touring in Saskatchewan some forty years later!

I'll have to wait to relate that.

Noah was another production by Leonard Crainford, who subsequently played a large part in launching my professional career.

The settings (Earth/Rain/Sun/Wind) for this fit-up touring were by that fine designer, Guy Sheppard, and he also composed and played for the incidental chants.

A man of many talents enhancing a wide range of drama throughout his career.

Mr and Mrs Noah were Jack Richman and Madeline Durrant; the three boys, Shem, Ham and Japheth, played by Henry F Wilkins, John Blain, and Howard Dickinson.

The three girls, Sella, Naomi and Ada were Iris Snowman, Margaret Godwin and Jane Kaye.

Several luminaries of the Company hid in the skins.

Frank OM Smith, the Bear, Kay Gardner, the Tiger, Janet Burrows, the Monkey, Maisie Dyke, the Cow (she was the producer's wife), Violet Rutter, the Lamb, Martin Summers, the Wolf, and Neil Wilson, the Elephant.

A great menagerie on the road.

Back in London for the Autumn season and involvement in a most unusual and (at that time) experimental production.

It was Hans Chlumberg's *Miracle at Verdun* (Trans: Edward Crankshaw)

A remarkable chronicle, especially at the time when the second world war was looming.

The staging called for

A Prologue' calling for twenty-nine characters.

'The Unknown Warriors Grave, Paris'. One character

'The War Memorial, Berlin', Two characters

'A Cemetery', Nineteen characters

'France' Two characters

'Germany', Two characters.

'England', Two characters.

'Verdun', Eight characters.

'Cornfield at Crossroads' (No characters)

'Cobblers shop/a village on the Snippe', Eleven characters

'German Inn', Eight characters.

'Quai D'Orsay, Paris', Twenty-one characters.

'The Cemetery' (again), 'Epilogue'. No characters.

More like a scenario for a movie.

However the Tavistock were not daunted by this saga of 57 actors (more than the original London production casting, where cardboard figures had been used in some cases), and the massive scene changes.

The *London Evening News* (October 19 1938), described this Miracle:

'*Miracle at Verdun* is a minor-miracle of production. This great play, which involves innumerable and rapid changes of locale and multitudinous cast is a spectacle that might well seem cramped at Drury Lane… Demands a mixture of acrobatics and necromancy. Technicians should go to the Tavistock to see Donald Hull's "projected" scenery used in this production. This method facilitated the 13 changes of scene. It is a method which may be revolutionary for impressionistic works'.

Out of the 86 characters, I played three roles,

Von Henkel, General von Gadenau and Kochler.

In this sort of galaxy, individual performances don't get much of a chance, but in that *London Evening News* review I was fortunate to get among the selected:

'The best of the performances came from Edward Wigand, Hudson Smith, Marjorie Withers and Leonard White…'

Other notable names in that melee were, Irene Palmer, John Blain, Michael Hitchman, Jane Burrows, Madeline Durrant, Iris Snowman, Frederick Spelling, Neil Pascall, Martin Benson, Sydney Green…

This extremely difficult major production was in the hands of Leonard Crainford, in association with Kay Gardner.

During all this involvement on the boards, fortunately – very fortunately – I was able to keep my relationship with Margaret growing daily between work in the City, the visits to Hounslow and the Thames-side walks.

I particularly remember one occasion when my enthusiasm led me to test my commitment and physical prowess!

Margaret with her family were taking a holiday in West Sussex with her grandmother who lived in Bersted, near Bognor Regis (renowned as 'Bugger Bognor'), and enjoying days on the beach. I made certain that I'd be visiting, home at Newhaven at the same time, bent on paying a surprise visit to Bognor beach one of those days.

It was a beautiful day, and fired by anticipation, I got on my bicycle and peddled off along the coast road from Newhaven to Bognor.

Phew!

Energy tested, but what wonderful luck when I, as though drawn by magic (or was it Eros?) easily found Margaret sitting on the end of a groyne, sunbathing...

Success. The ache in my limbs vanished.

The sight was stunning.

I was so glad that I'd taken my camera, but that vision remains in my memory fresher than the print.

Later, sadly, going home, although re-charged, the bike-ride was less energetic. I lost all enthusiasm for the ride. Getting near Brighton, I gave up, rang my father to assure him that I was ok, and told him that I was going to finish the journey on the train. No longer impelled as I was at the start of the day.

But, it was especially good though to carry that memory picture with me; and not a bad picture from my Box Brownie as well.

**

Now into the fateful year of 1939. Peace or War?

The Tavistock Repertory Company greeted the New Year with a Pantomime. *Dick Whittington*, but with a difference, described as an 'Edwardian pantomimical extravaganza'. Frank Harwood wrote the book and lyrics, and also Produced. (Jan 6, 1939)

For me another complete contrast from *Miracle at Verdun* and the German roles I played in that.

Variety being one of the strong blessings of Repertory in training then.

In the panto I played Demon Rat and occupied stage-left of course. (The baddies are always the best parts!)

The Times (Jan 7, 1939), on the one hand, considered it...

'It is practically impossible to burlesque a pantomime... but as it is Mr Frank Harwood does his best.'

And on the other hand, The Stage (Jan 12, 1939),

'Credit is due to Frank Harwood, the producer, for a well-presented show…with an extra word of commendation for Leonard White for his work as Demon Rat.

Dorothy Fox played the Principal Boy, John Blain, Alderman Fitzwarren, Hugh Evans, Sarah, the cook, Jack Newmark and Henry F Wilkins, "Two asinine apprentices".

After the Christmas season we presented the morality play *Everyman* (probably 16th century). This version had been performed by the Ben Greet Players at St Anne's Soho a year before, with Ernest Milton playing Everyman.

Tavistock's presentation was produced by Osmond P Raphael, and was notable for having John Wyse playing the lead, and for having the Mass composed by Edric Cundell, sung by students of the Guildhall School of Music preceding the drama.

Guy Sheppard designed the setting and costumes.

I played Fellowship.

And then at Eastertime that year, I was invited to join another company – The Centaur Players, who were presenting in Wimbledon, John Masefield's verse play *Good Friday*, with, as a curtain-raiser, *Sister Gold* (from the *Little Plays of St Francis* by Laurence Housman).

Apart from feeling good insofar that I was sought to play elsewhere, and with a different Company, it was very attractive to have the chance to perform Masefield's powerful verse, and that, as it happened, strengthened a line of my work later.

I played Longinus the Centurion who has that wonderful speech describing to Pontius Pilate the crucifixion of Christ.

A speech that has echoed in my memory ever since.

'the best piece of acting came from Leonard White when, as Longinus, the Centurion, he described the death of Christ on Calvary. He held his audience throughout a dramatic passage ably and movingly delivered.' (*The Stage*, April 13, 1939)

Paul M Beney played Pilate, Kitty Tenison, Procula, his wife.

F Shenton Kilshawe directed both plays. He also played St Francis in Housman's *Sister Gold*. In that I played The Miser.

Not 'popular theatre', but I was very glad to have the opportunity to work with such special talents as the Masefield and Housman creations. All too rare.

I quickly rejoined Tavistock Rep for their Spring season which presented five productions of GB Shaw plays. I was in three between April and May.

First was *Androcles and the Lion* (Apr 28, 1939) produced by Raymond Raikes. I played the role of The Captain opposite Edith Rose as Lavinia.

Much later in my career I Directed this play with the students at the London Academy of Music & Dramatic Art (LAMDA).

But, next at the Tavistock, the rarely performed Shaw's first play, *Widowers' Houses*. (May 19, 1939). Produced by Vincent Pearmain, and described as having "undeniable merits as an engaging satire on contemporary life and as the earliest manifestation of a caustic pen, which has influenced the whole course of British drama."

Only seven in this cast, and I was able to get my teeth into the leading part of Dr. Harry Trench.

Also playing were Rowland F White (no relation), Margaret Godwin, Jack Newmark, Wilfred Sultan, Olive Willis and Martin Benson.

'Leonard White played Harry Trench well, successfully surviving the switch from the burlesque of the earlier scenes to the sincerity of the latter' (*The Stage* 25/5/39).

In no less than a week later Tavistock presented a big cast in *Caesar and Cleopatra* (May 26/39). Production by Raymond Raikes. John Blain played Caesar and June Grimble, Cleopatra (aged 16).

New names with us were Greta Gjeruldsen (Ftatateeta), Yvonne de Leddra (Charmian) and Eric Wynn Owen (Ptolemy).

After my lead in the previous show I relaxed in the small role of Belzanor – the Syrian Warrior.

Fourteen years after writing this play, Shaw had added a prologue spoken by the Egyptian God Ra, but time did not allow us to include this. Excerpts were, however, printed in the programme…

'the two thousand years that have passed, are to me, the God Ra, but a moment; nor is this day any other than the day in which Caesar set foot in the land of my people...'

Next came my second tour to South Wales (July 1939), and as it turned out my last production with the Tavistock.

World events intervened.

We did one of JB Priestley's *Time* plays – *I Have Been Here Before.*

As before we played Trealaw (Rhondda), Pontypridd, Maesteg, and Bargoed, adding new venues at Tavarnaubach and Merthyr Tydfil.

And again a wide variety of stages, ranging from thousand-seaters to much smaller ones, even still using gas lighting!

Guy Sheppard designed, and Desmond Hall built to cope in what was described as his 'expanding suitcase' plan.

The cast included Gwendolen Bacon, Jack Richman, Frank OM Smith (who also directed the tour, before taking over all his work at London's Arts Theatre), Madeline Durrant, and John Blain.

I played Sam Shipley. A character role, calling for Wig by Gustave and Yorkshire accent by me.

Thankfully it worked. Great training.

Leonard Crainford produced.

A future Director, Ethel Smith, was our Stage-Manager at that time.

Only a few weeks after that Mr Chamberlain was telling us that 'we were at war with Germany', and the first air-raid sirens were heard galvanising us all into another world we knew not what...

But strangely it was an immediate period of eerie calm.

For me I lost my job. CWJ Miller & Co's German trade, was stopped. I knew that I'd be 'called up for service', but unsure of how long before that would happen.

I started to search the job columns of *The Stage* newspaper.

It might be a holding period when I just might try to make the professional leap?

Experimental?

I saw an advert for the Alexandra Theatre, South Shields – The Premier Drama Stock Theatre of the North – as it was described, and I applied.

Their response was –

October 11th 1939: Alexandra Theatre, South Shields

Dear Sir:

Re yours of the 28th ultimo can offer you £2.10 shillings per week, juvenile lead at the above. Rehearse Tuesday 17th inst., open 23rd.,

One play per week. Usual fortnight's notice on either side.

Yours faithfully,

pp Hird & Elwes

It was 'twice-nightly'!

While I was dithering, Margaret rescued me. I don't know if she knew of my move North possibility, but I hope it might have been that she did, and didn't want me to go.

But, whatever, and happily she got me a job at the same firm of Chartered Accounts (Jocelyne, Miles & Page in King Street in the City) where she then worked.

Figuring again.

Two blessings. A welcome temporary employment and especially, especially it kept us together. We were even put on assignments together, Auditing accounts in big firms around the country. One in particular, which took us to Worcester for several days, is very memorable.

Also during that time, Margaret came with me to be introduced to my Mother and Father and stay at Newhaven. I particularly wanted my Mum to see her. I also wanted to show her the lovely South Downs where I had taken long walks over the years, and to see the harbour and the boats and the Channel. Show-off a bit.

Being impressive with my enthusiasm was one thing, but taking a twenty mile hike in our stride, up hill and down dale, was perhaps straining it a bit for a girl only used to Wimbledon Common, Hounslow Heath, and the Thames riverside.

But I was overjoyed that we were growing together in these uncertain times.

The Tavistock Little Theatre had now ceased production, and before getting our call-up notices, a few of ex-members decided to get together for a last time.

One, Patrick Leinster organised and produced a special one-off performance of *Othello* to be given on a Sunday in the Grafton Theatre, February 18, 1940.

That Theatre was a small modern venue that had been built under the new hotel at the top of Tottenham Court Road. It was licensed to Actor David Farrar who was running it for a series of plays starring himself. He was playing Captain Banner (George R Preedy) at that time.

We were called the AVA Players. I don't know why?

The cast included, Madeline Durrant, Kay Joseph, John Cain, Patrick Leinster, Edward Wigand, Reginald Matthews, Douglas Snelgar, Stanley Beard, Malya Nappi, John Persson.

I was playing Othello, believe it or not!

Not exactly the role for me at age 24. I was much too young (and inexperienced).

However it was a play that Patrick Leinster (the Director) wanted very much to do and for me to play the lead.

And he to play Iago.

So the moment and the challenge persuaded me.

I had a go. No one complained.

Backstage credits included:

The Set adapted from a design by Raymond Raikes.

Constructed by Betty Upton.

The Stage-Manager was Ethel Smith.

Margaret joined in to help with the panotrope (playing the music effects/records). It all helped, but I think, under the circumstances, it was a first and a last for her!

And I can understand that.

Poised as I was to get my 'call-up', and faced with the question direct, I promised Margaret that I would not look for an Acting career after the war.

Things changed radically when eventually my call-up papers arrived.

Chapter Three

All the world's a stage...

Under the 'National Service (Armed Forces) Act 1939, I was called for a Medical to be examined at Upper Holloway Hall, Holloway Road London N1 on the 19th March 1940.

I was described as

A Man, Age 23 +134 days,

Height 5ft 9 and a half inches.

Eyes: Blue.

Hair Colour: Brown.

GRADE: 1 (One)

Surprise, surprise!

Thus catalogued, Registered HRF 5244, my Enlistment Notice dated April 11 1940 called upon me for Service on April 18 1940. For the 'Duration of the Emergency'.

Goodbye, 54 Wilberforce Road Finsbury Park, London N4.

I was posted to the Royal Berkshire Regiment and told to report to Brock Barracks, Reading.

Off with the "civvies" and on with the rough khaki.

Away with the leisurely amble and into the smart 'Left, right: left, right: left, right… Pick 'em up lad!'

'Get yer hair cut.'

Away with the soft shoe shuffle and into the heavy boots.

Those boots!

'I want those toe-caps polished so you can see yer face in 'em!'

Spit and polish. 'Stand by yer beds!'

Six weeks basic Infantry training. Regimental history,

Square-bashing, rifle drill, bayonet thrusting into straw "bodies"!

Strangely, among the Rookies I did not take this complete change too terribly. I think I tried to treat it in the same sort of unreality as it might be in playing a different role. I had to play a soldier, change of costume and all that. But of course that didn't last long. It WAS for real.

I was now Private, LG White, No 5343035. Grade A1.

Six weeks "hard".

Unexpectedly, I got my first stripe – appointed Lance Corporal on June 21, 1940. So my audition must have gone ok. Then a short respite, a 48 hour pass to go home.

I went back to Newhaven transformed.

A role quite unlike any other and for which I was quite unprepared.

Returning after that leave I was transferred to nearby Reading-Ranikhet Camp at Tilehurst.

I was classified as a Signaller (Infantry) on 3rd September 1940, and promoted to Corporal on November 22nd, and expected to be posted to a Battalion.

But that didn't happen, and instead I was retained and sent on a Wireless course at 55 Division Signals (January 19, 1941).

Later, when the Royal Air Force badly needed recruitment the call went out to training establishments of the infantry that men could transfer to the RAF.

I thought that this was my chance. I very much wanted to fly. Several of my pals at Tilehurst applied and were accepted, so I also applied for it, full of high hopes of becoming a pilot.

I was very disappointed when my CO of HQ Company,

Lieutenant (later Captain) Hewlett refused to submit my application. He said that as I was by now a trainer myself and that he couldn't let me go.

Deflation.

I had no realisation of it at the time – I was only full of disappointment – but in retrospect it was, of course, a decision that probably lengthened my life.

I was sent to Catterick to attend a Course to become a Regimental Signals Instructor, and greatly to my surprise I was qualified Distinguished.

A welcome bonus during that six weeks in North Yorkshire was to discover that lovely Georgian Playhouse at Richmond, and to be able to get to see performances there.

Three years later I managed to get back to that School of Signals at Catterick (December 1944) to attend another Instruction Course. Only briefly that time, but good to be close to Richmond theatre again, and keep in touch with that other world … Curtain Up.

Before that though, I was destined to stay based near Reading for some two years, and I was lucky to make contact with the Reading Repertory Company, (known as the 70 Theatre in London Street) and luckier still to be able to practise my acting, and avoid getting rusty (the end of the war "by Christmas" had long since gone).

I was first of all cast as Charles Randolph in Dodie Smith's *Dear Octopus*. Another example marking the difference between what was acceptable in those days, and what now.

There I was, certainly not cast to type, 24 years old and playing a white-haired character celebrating 50 years of married life! Stretching the imagination considerably.

But it seemed to have been acceptable.

Suspension of disbelief, and all that.

'Another acquisition (to the Company) is Leonard White who wears a beard and an air of philosophical submission as the other golden-wedding partner.' (*Berkshire Chronicle* April 18, 1941.)

Next, something quite different, and at least nearer my age, Ashley Dukes' *The Man With a Load of Mischief*.

'Credit must be given to Leonard White for the outstanding way he took the part of his man…' (*Reading Standard*, June 6, 1941.)

'Leonard White, as his servant, commands the stage with his impersonation of a lackey, who would much better fill his master's position.' (*Berkshire Chronicle* June 6, 1941.)

Good fortune continued with these opportunities.

Journeys into the unreal – escapism – while the days, and nights, of air-raids continued in our back-yards.

Actually, Margaret's back-yard in Hounslow was more in the bombing-line than we were in Reading. The civilians getting the worst of it while we in the Army, who ought to have been the targets, were seemingly ignored.

Many were the nights when I'd be sitting in my signals truck on a "Yellow Peril Alert", frustrated, while watching reflected in the clouds in the east, over London, the hellish fires and bomb explosions. Whereas if I just looked skywards above Reading, it would be starlit and quiet.

Weird.

Gut-wrenching, uselessness.

During all this horror, Margaret bravely, like so many others, still relentlessly continued each morning to make the journey to work. She, from Hounslow East on the Piccadilly Line into the City, picking her way through the debris and rubble and the still burning buildings, to see if the work still existed.

Margaret's did.

In spite of all, another bonus for me at this time, a real joy, was that at weekends Margaret was able to visit me at Tilehurst.

The Green Line coach service was, remarkably, still running and not such a long journey from the Bath Road in Hounslow to Reading. Apart from her lovely self she would bring "goodies". We would picnic. One of our favourite walks was into the woods of nearby Maple Durham.

Those wonderful meetings, so contrasted with the daily horrors elsewhere, seemed to turn their reality into happy dreams. But so fortunately they were for real.

Our courting was for keeps.

I managed to do one more play for the Reading Rep.

On Oct 20th 1941, we opened in Jerome K Jerome's *The Soul of Nicholas Snyders*. I played the lead.

A good cast, directed by Bill Bristow with a pro-am mix and a standard that enabled me with peculiar good fortune to add to my experience which I'd had with the Tavistock Theatre Company in London before the war started.

'Leonard White as Nicholas Snyders carries his audience along with him. His articulation is perfect and the quality of his acting outstanding.' (*Reading Standard.*)

The Bristow family became good friends and indeed played host to Margaret when she was visiting me and able to stay-over.

Courting days were coming to a happy climax. Margaret was nearing her 21st birthday, and in the old-fashioned way, "coming of age". That was important because, just before the War, there was an unhappy period when our relationship had been broken. Her parents had warned me off, and I thought my hopes were dashed.

But, extraordinarily, and I mean extraordinarily, quite some time later, a miracle happened..

I was wasting away a Sunday evening in my Finsbury Park digs when the phone rang.

I took the call, and very happily immediately recognised the voice on the other end. The voice told me 'It's all right now, you can come down…'

Nothing more and no time for explanations.

As fast as my legs and the London Underground would carry me, I was on my way, Finsbury Park to Hounslow East and on to Ellerdine Road; a well-worn journey in the past. Full of the joys of Spring I was soon knocking at the door of *Balure* (Margaret's home name).

Soon the door was opened by her Mother, who looked very surprised and actually addressed me as Nigel.

I ignored that.

That was corrected, thankfully, and I was told to come in. I don't remember much detail of what followed, but it had no sense of being strained, just unexpected.

However, this is the extraordinary – and I mean extraordinary, part of it. Margaret said later that she had never made the phone call to me, 'It's all right now, you can come down…'!

So, a complete mystery.

A mystery phone-call that I completely assumed was Margaret speaking, and it wasn't.

A mystery phone-call that completely changed my life.

Margaret was twenty-one years old on February 26, 1942 and we were married just two days later, on February 28, 1942, at St Stephen's Church, Hounslow.

I remember it for, at least, three reasons.

First for the remarkable incident that brought us together again; secondly for the wonderful happiness, and thirdly for the fact that the Vicar charged us twice for the ceremony.

I had paid in advance, but on the day he got it all again from my best man, my Bro-in-law (sister Alice's husband, Lawrence Hibling).

We didn't ask for a refund.

The event was compatible with wartime fare and conditions. I got seven days Privilege leave from February 27.

I was in my uniform. Margaret in a lovely light-blue dress for the service and then (it was February) an attractive fur coat (artificial of course) for travel. And the sun came out, cheering-up a winter wartime day.

To this day – well over sixty years later – a section of that same coat covers the back seat of our car.

We have worn well!

Everything comes in useful.

The reception, back at Margaret's home, was a small gathering, enjoying rations that had been carefully gathered from contributions saved for the special day.

We didn't miss at all the peacetime "do" and knees-up.

It was all much appreciated by those at table – Grannie Kent (Margaret's paternal grandmother), my Dad and Mother, my sister Alice and husband Lawrence Hibling (he had done his duty as best man at short notice because my Army pal (Ben Harrison) from Tilehurst Camp who had intended to be with me, elected to get married himself on that same day! It was catching in those days). Also, young Barrymore, (my first nephew) and Margaret's young brother, Roger; Margaret's cousin,

Joan Rexworthy who was serving in the WRAF stationed in London, and, of course, my new father and mother-in-law, Margaret's mother and father, Edward Kent and Ethel (Hawkins).

The honeymoon was short but so special amid the overhanging wartime.

A meal for just us at the (then) famous restaurant, underground at the Regent Cinema, in Brighton – in the days when cinemas were "Palaces"; followed by two nights at Stroods Hotel in the village of Sayers Common, just a few miles north of the South Downs.

Two nights there cost £2-12s-10d. (I've still got the bill.)

All too soon, the Army re-called to Tilehurst Camp, and Margaret went back to her home, the City and her work and the bombing.

We hadn't set up any home of our own yet. There wasn't much point.

We continued getting together as much as we could up and down the Great West Road. Always against the odds of the air-raids.

Two further memories linger. One visit to Hounslow when I had to sleep – or try to – under the dining room table during a raid. That was where the Morrison shelter would have been if they'd had one. The rest of the family were in the Anderson shelter in the garden. There wasn't room for me out there.

Another occasion was when I was in the black-out walking along the Great West Road, hoping to catch the Green Line bus back to Reading (we were always optimistic).

Actually it wasn't in the black-out because it was during an air-raid and fire-bombs were dropping and lighting up the whole area. They seemed to be getting too close for comfort, and in some sort of desperation I had to drop to the ground in the gutter, and stay there for a while.

I think that was the closest I ever got to the firing-line during the whole of my six years that I was in the Army.

There was another surprising near-miss, come to think of it, when Margaret and I were visiting family at Newhaven.

It was a lovely day and we were taking a pleasant countryside walk near Bullon's Bush (that's what we called it). Quiet and peaceful. That is, it was, until we heard a plane high and distant.

We couldn't see it, and so continued enjoying our walk undisturbed. Probably one of ours. We were always optimistic.

Suddenly, a plop in the long grass nearby, stopped us in our tracks. We froze.

All around us bullets were dropping.

Frightening.

We still couldn't see any plane, and then after getting over the initial fright, we came to the conclusion that, fortunately, the 'missiles' were only spent ammunition.

Certainly, sighs of relief.

Scary nevertheless.

By now, the something like two years I'd been at the Tilehurst Training Camp as a Signals Instructor came to an end, when it was decided to amalgamate the training faculties for both the Royal Berkshire Regiment and the Royal Sussex Regiment, and base us in a new Unit at Colchester Barracks.

Very sad in that Margaret was, then, further away and not able to visit me as often. However it might have been very much worse. Many, many more of the chaps of my call-up were abroad on active service.

My war was still cushy by comparison. But I had no choice in the matter. The unplanned theme continued…

As at Reading, now in Colchester I was happy to find the Rep Theatre going strongly. Unfortunately it wasn't so easy to get the chances to arrange my free time to enable me to get into productions there. But, I did enjoy hanging around the theatre, meeting Artistic Director, Digby-Day, his staff and company; keeping in touch with civvy street, as best I could.

After a while I did get very near to getting something going. Through the Vicar of the Church nearby, I suggested that a production combining the Rep and the Church might be worth investigating.

I suggested putting together John Masefield's verse play *Good Friday* and Stainer's oratorio, *The Crucifixion*. The play for the theatre company and the music for the Church choir as a special production for Easter.

Lots of enthusiasm but, alas, it never got off the ground. The Army had other ideas for me.

I got twice into situations where I ought to have been in line for more active service.

First being posted to a Battalion being formed in Northern Ireland prior to going overseas.

We were in Donaghadee.

My Signals HQ was in a lovely house by the seaside. Under the circumstances the digs were excellent. Apart from duties I amused myself by creating a "Wall Newspaper" in our HQ, which I called *Look*. Not exactly *Picture Post*, but doubtless influenced by that magazine.

And we were looked after by the locals very well.

My library still hosts a copy of a book of poems *Songs of the Port* by WHF Patterson, who lived in Donaghadee at that time, and which was given to me by Jean, when I left her home town. It had been her own personal gift from the poet to her.

There was a rumour that we were being kitted for Norway? The calm before the storm? But, contrary, the build-up, without any seeming reason, stopped.

After all that preparation it came to naught. The Battalion was disbanded, broken up, without any explanation and we all went back to our various units. A period of limbo.

A second move towards the front line happened when, not long after, I was again posted to another Battalion being formed.

This time – again at the seaside – in East Anglia.

It was spread over parts of Suffolk, but my Signals HQ was set up in a commandeered private house almost on the seashore in Walberswick. Under any other circumstances than the war, a wonderful haven. I was billeted in another private house nearby.

Again the unreal contrast of the idyllic and the horrific potential. On the one hand, Margaret was able to visit me and stay in my billet. In the most easy-going way I was able to get up at the crack of dawn, get into my PT kit and go and do the daily exercises with the platoon, and then return to my billet and back to bed with Margaret until eventually rising at a respectable hour for breakfast, and then duty.

Southwold was only a short row-boat-ferry away across the river for the town amenities.

And to crown it, Walberswick had a lovely private theatre in the garden of Ronald Jeans, the playwright.

No activity there unfortunately in which to get involved, but my, by now, deep interest as an actor, meant that I was made very welcome. And a plus included invitations to tea at the fine house.

All that contrasted so sharply with the reminders of the darker horrors around us.

Being in my signals office on alert on the long day and all night when our first thousand bomber raid took place. The incessant drone of that endless stream of our planes passing overhead, crossing the coast out over the North Sea, and indeed bombers returning after their raids had been completed, while fresh planes were still leaving on their missions.

And I saw my first dead body of the war, and my only one, washed up on the seashore. It might have been in the water for some while. It was only a torso. One of ours or one of theirs? Impossible to tell. One of those airmen perhaps? Horribly impersonal, fried, or boiled.

Thousands may die, but each one is a whole world.

Earth-time stopped.

Again after the build-up ready for some sort of overseas service, and going where we knew not, it wasn't long before again, without any explanation the Battalion was disbanded and back again I went to the Training unit!

Was it something I said?

But, it wasn't for long.

Out of the blue (in 1943) I was posted to join the staff of the 160 Support Group (Heavy Mortars & MG) OCTU (Officer Cadet Training Unit) based at Alton Towers in Staffordshire (one of Lord Salisbury's residences).

I certainly got some impressive billets.

Made up to Lance Sergeant and then quickly to War Substantive Sergeant, I was then in the entirely unexpected role of training Officer-Cadets in Signals for their units.

The make-up of the OCTU staff was from a mix of Regiments and formed a world unto itself.

Hard and very strict.

The Cadets were given a much tougher time than I'd seen handed out to rookies in the ranks at my earlier training units.

The Commandant was from the Middlesex Regiment.

He marked his persona by appearing on parade dressed in jodhpurs, wearing yellow gloves and always carrying a whip which he delighted in swishing threateningly and slapping his legs…

I thought he might have been auditioning for Erich Von Stroheim roles. Except of course he wasn't. He was for real.

The Adjutant (Capt. Smith) was thankfully a lot more human. He had an association with Stratford-upon-Avon (I believe, pre-war, he had been a teacher at the Grammar School) and, later on, it transpired, he had great interest in my being with the Memorial Theatre there.

Also my HQ Company Commander, was a descendent of the famous Lucy family, who had an association with the Shakespeare country insofar that he was, ancestrally from Charlecote Park.

Again (in 1946) when I was at the Memorial Theatre, the Company were invited to visit that ancestral home for tea, by my old Company Commander. He was tickled pink to find me acting with the Shakespeare Company.

Another among the motley crew at Alton Towers I can't forget (who could?), was the Regimental Sergeant Major. A splendid Guardsman, tough and very very rarely seen to be off-duty. He could spend a considerable time in the Sergeants' Mess bar, showing all the other Sergeants he was the toughest, knocking 'em back, and then excusing himself temporarily, while he'd go and take Guard Parade, as sober as a judge, then return hat off and stick down, to resume to find out who was buying the next round.

Hard as nails on duty, a strict disciplinarian, not one to cross, but strangely for a guy like me interested in Acting (we'd all be "nancies" to him), I got on with him quite well. He used to prefer me to take over the office on any occasion when he couldn't be in charge.

I think that he regarded the Signals lot as something a bit special. He was not understanding all that wireless stuff.

And so treated us with some respect.

Surprise, surprise, a few years later, after the end of the war, I happened to be walking in Liverpool, when I was shocked to see that same man standing in another uniform, as a Commissionaire, outside a Cinema there.

He was as shocked as I was.

After the initial surprise, a difficult pause, only a few words were spoken.

I felt he was not really pleased to be found in those so changed circumstances.

So sad. Power diminished.

But back at Alton Towers, before that, the training pattern continued. I had a room in the main building, and so reasonably comfortable. The cadets were all in temporary huts built in the grounds, which in the winter were only heated by small stoves. It wasn't unusual on cold nights to find those stoves red hot and dangerously close to the bottom of nearby bunks.

In spite of warnings the inevitable happened. One night I was awakened by a fire-alarm and looking out of my room window saw one of the huts well ablaze. Thankfully no one was seriously injured.

Each intake of cadets included in their training, tactical exercises, for which we moved to Mid Wales, Radnorshire. We (Signals) were based in Rhayader.

Again, a nice house right on the side of the river by the bridge. But under battle conditions for the cadets only little time was spent in Rhayader. Most of it was up in the mountains.

I still feel the chill of the coldest night I've ever spent huddled in a drafty 15cwt. truck, on listening watch, on a 22-set (or was it a No.11?) at the top of a bleak peak on one of those occasions. Most of the time reception ruined by the moving "Heaviside layer", and my hands too frozen to adjust the dials… Thankfully it wasn't for real.

But I do have warm memories of the hospitality we received in Rhayader.

Gertrude Evans ran a baker's shop there (lovely cakes) and welcomed us.

And apart from the so good food extras, I can still hear way back in my sound memory those lovely Welsh voices.

So, for me, visits to our "war games" were always made bearable – actually, attractive – by Gertrude and her daughter Phyllis.

Even after the war, Phyllis visited Margaret and me when we lived in North London, and we have kept in contact, albeit usually only on the Festive occasions, ever since.

The only expression of my entertaining self while at 160 OCTU, Alton Towers, was at the occasional social or concert in the NAAFI; I never got any drama going. But I took every opportunity to put shows together. I quite enjoyed playing MC and seeking out talent for ad hoc Variety nights.

At this time I discovered that my old Tavistock Rep Producer, Leonard Crainford, had joined CEMA (Council for the Encouragement of Music and Arts, the precursor of the Arts Council) and was in an office in the Stoke-on-Trent area organising professional tours in the Midlands. So I certainly made contact with him again and occasionally was able to get to see some of those touring shows. They were largely music based and of high standard.

Sometimes we were blessed with a visit by a few of those groups to Alton Towers itself.

Apart from that, special highlights were on the few occasions, when Margaret could get to visit me at Alton and stay locally. All too rare.

Precious.

My most important memory of those days at 160 OCTU was one day when I happened to be in our Signals Office (I was pottering, mending something) when a telegram arrived and it was for me!

In those days for me telegrams usually only meant one of two things. Either cheering first-night greetings or else bad news.

Well, I certainly didn't have any opening night to celebrate, so some trepidation to experience.

I took a deep breath and moved towards the ATS Operator at the switchboard.

She was smiling!

'Here you are Sergeant.'

She handed me the message. It hadn't even had time to be put into the familiar envelope...

I read....

```
To: Sgt White, Royal Berkshire Regiment
Martin arrived 7.45am 6 1/4 lbs. Both well.
Mum.
```

It was February 1st 1944. (My mother's birthday!

Years later mother always said that Margaret had done it specially for her...)

Words failed me then and they still do. Well, almost.

Our first baby was born.

A boy. Martin Guy...

I don't think I could finish the job I was on. I was off like a flash to the Company office to see how quickly I could get away to see Margaret and the lad at 298 Ellerdine Road Hounslow East.

And the start of a truly rich blessing.

***

Back to earth only a few days later, and picking up the routine at Alton Towers. But now without doubt a new meaning to things – even to the war.

The future now had added focus.

While keeping my ears open for any opportunities to be able to see Margaret and baby Martin, I came to hear that a drama group had been set up in London, under the War Office no less.

Extraordinary!

It was headed by Michael Macowan, the famous theatre Director, now a Major in the Army, and with Stephen Murray, that splendid leading actor.

It sounded very strange. I couldn't understand it at all?

It had a very civil service title of *The Army Bureau of Current Affairs Play Unit*. No kidding!

It was administered by the Central Pool of Artistes.

No harm done I thought, I'll apply to find out more and to see if I can join.

I soon found out that I couldn't join. A letter from Major Michael Macowan, from his office in Eaton Square (impressive address) SW1, told me that the Unit was only made up of personnel unfit for active service (graded C3s and below).

As I was still graded A1 and thereby available for transfer to active duty, I was not allowed to join his Play Unit.

But he would keep me in mind if the circumstances changed..

So I continued training the Officer-Cadets at Alton Towers and hoped that somehow circumstances would change.

Eventually they did. VE Day happened.

God be praised the pressure was released somewhat.

True, the terrible war still went on in the Far East. VJ Day certainly remained unforeseen.

But it did mean that the constrictions previously in place regarding recruitment to the ABCA Play Unit were relaxed.

They could now form a second company, including A1's.

I got my chance.

Full of the joys, I went to report to an office of the Central Pool of Artistes, in Soho, of which my only memory, is when on looking at the Orders Board in the entrance hall, I saw that Private P Ustinov was listed as being on Fire Duty on Christmas Day.

I've wondered since whether he might have thought that lucky or unlucky? Perhaps he volunteered?

An opportunity for his pen?

Christmas Day in Soho – with all the strip-joints on holiday? Perhaps not.

Then I went to meet the Major Michael Macowan in Eaton Square. An imposing house, and his office a very large room.

Opening the door echoed through the empty space, bare, except for the one very large table across the far corner with only one chair behind it.

Michael Macowan was a small man (physically, I mean) And it took me a few moments to focus on him.

When I did, I was surprised to find him perched in the chair, not sitting in it. The impression was of a small bird – a sparrow – or perhaps more like a little owl – sizing me up.

I couldn't believe my good fortune in getting into this unusual play unit while I was still in the Army. And here I was to be working with one of the finest theatre Directors, in London. Also while I was expecting the usual interview and 'we'll let you know later' sort of thing, there was nothing of that. It all seemed to be accepted that I was joining without question!

I felt good.

I learnt that I was the first to join of this second company (the original under Stephen Murray was performing abroad somewhere…), and as I was a Sergeant I'd likely look after the organisation as necessary.

I was to go and get myself sorted out with a billet and 'keep in touch'!

Getting myself sorted out with a billet, was such a marvellous bonus with this posting. Now I could actually live "at home".

As soon as Margaret knew of my good fortune she set about finding a home for us. In, no time at all, and with some help from my cousin (Jessie) in Wilberforce Road N4 (my pre-war digs) she found an apartment in the same road at No 29.

It consisted really of just a few rooms at the top of the Victorian terrace house. Two rooms, sitting/dining and one bedroom on the top floor, then down one flight of stairs to a small kitchen on a landing, then down another short staircase to a shared toilet. The cast-iron bath hung on the wall on the staircase.

Nothing self-contained about that!

Nevertheless it was our first home. Great.

Margaret and young Martin (now just coming up to starting infant school, which he did at Blackstock Road) and me, we moved in.

I was still in the Army, I was anticipating working in some sort of Theatre (I was not sure what?) and now all together as a family living at home in London.

Albeit still war-torn, but Fate was being very kind to me.

Unbelievable it was, at a time when anything but that was more the norm for the very many PBI ("Poor bloody infantry") in those elongated years of wartime.

Activity at the ABCA Play Unit at first was slow to build.

New members got posted only one or two at a time.

Notably, the actor, now Private Andre van Gyseghem (husband of Jean Forbes Robertson) was early to arrive.

He had obviously been earmarked to lead the second Company, because it was only a very short time before he left us and in no time at all returned with pips on his shoulders – now an Officer!

While we were waiting the full team to assemble, a small group of us – some seven or eight – put together several tours giving lectures and play-readings. All in the best intentions of education and preparation for civvy street.

A general title might have been *Theatre and Life*.

Lectures illustrated in dramatic form, hopefully to provoke enlivened discussion.

These 'events' were generally given during parade hours to AA (Anti-aircraft) and Searchlight units, and (surprisingly perhaps) proved very popular.

Largely due, I think, to the element of pleasant surprise.

A novel way of being on Parade.

The average Gunner reading his Orders of the Day and seeing an ABCA period of about one-and-a- half hours devoted to some lectures on Theatre was not likely to be very impressed. But, his/her apathy invariably changed to distinct enthusiasm when the entertainment was revealed.

This first presentation was lead by Andre van Gyseghem to start with but taken over by me while "Van" was away being changed into an Officer.

Excerpts to enliven the lecture were taken from such plays as *Waiting for Lefty* (Odets), *Widowers' Houses* (Shaw), *Distant Point* (Affinogenev), *An Enemy of the People* (Ibsen) and *The Drunkard* (Anonymous).

During this period of formation of the Unit, these "illustrated lectures" were also given at Universities under the auspices of Courses organised by Army Personnel.

A touch of quality? Art in planning for Peace, perhaps?

We also ran a very interesting Week-end Drama School at Lowestoft. It was organised at a Royal Artillery HQ, at which personnel attended from over a large area.

Some forty or fifty Officers and other ranks of both sexes assembled on a Friday for three and a half days, spent under exceedingly congenial conditions (would civvy street ever be as nice as this?).

The syllabus included, production and acting classes (Clifford Evans and Anthony Blake conducted these), play-readings, discussions, a "Brains Trust". Van Gyseghem lectured on the Russian Theatre, and there was a visit to the Maddermarket Theatre in Norwich.

That programme we toured from June to August (1945) covering 21 varied venues throughout the country.

By September, the full Company of the ABCA Play Unit second unit, had been assembled. There had been many difficulties, not the least being the drafting of two VADs (Voluntary Nursing). Those girls had first to be discharged from the Nursing Service, then re-enlisted into the ATS, and then posted to ABCA…

The Company were:

Capt Andre van Gyseghem

Lieut Michael Langham (who had just been released from a POW Camp)

BSM Nat Brenner (Eventually being most notable and successful for running the Bristol Old Vic Theatre School)

Sgt Alan Badel

Sgt Ninian Brodie

Sgt John Gay

Sgt Leonard White

Bdr Anthony Blake

Bdr Charles McFie

Pte Richard Davies

Pte Norman Driver (later Norman Mitchell)

Pte Clifford Evans

Pte Percy Roberts

Rfn Geoffrey Colville

Spr William Eedle

Pte Charles Houston

Pte Alastair Duncan

Pte Jack Jackson

Pte Gwylam Edwards (later Meredith Edwards)

Cpl Margaret Courtney

Pte Enid Drummond-Young

Pte Barbara Greenhalgh

Pte Lilian Moran

Pte Christine Russell

Our writers included Ted Willis, Senior Comdr. Bridget Boland, Christopher Hassall, and Sgn. Jack Lindsay; Composer, Berkeley Fase; Designer, Leslie Hurrey; Painter, Alick Johnstone.

What a cast!

We now went on the road with two original plays that had been specially written for the first Company.

A double bill *Two Plays of the Moment.*

Where Do We Go From Here? (by Bridget Boland and Ted Willis, with verse interludes by Jack Lindsay).

Planning For Peace. In that I played the Member of Parliament.

The second play was *The Great Swap* (by Ted Willis and Jack Lindsay) 'Something quite different – an original and amusing treatise on Lend-Lease – the cooperation of the Allies'.

In that I doubled as the Chinese Officer and Greek Man.

They were documentary style "Living Newspaper" creations. Introducing a new form for Theatre.

We opened with a preview given specially for 'the biz' in London, at the Arts Theatre, of which Merton Hodge (*The Telegraph*) wrote:

'It was most enthusiastically received by a house of critical West-end actors, managers and critics.....It is the best afternoon's entertainment and lesson I have had in the London theatre for a very long time, and is presented in the best Theatre Guild (USA) tradition. Anyone who does not see it is missing something significant of the times in which we have lived, are living now, and will possibly live in the future'.

This tour was presented by The Arts Council early in its transformation from being CEMA, (Council for the Encouragement of Music and the Arts), and now headed by Michael MacOwan after his demob, and continuing his connection with the ABCA Play Unit.

We played between October 2 and November 5, 1945 at eight further venues, which included five days in each of two venues – Bradford and Llandrindod Wells.

We continued after a short break with a change of double bill. Instead of *The Great Swap* we put in *The Bomb's All Yours* (by Senior Commander Bridget Boland – freely adapted from a radio play by Horton and Ann Giddy.

The lyric of *Hello Fission* by Christopher Hassall, with accompaniment composed by Berkeley Fase).

A brave subject to tackle at that time. About the A-bomb, no less. I found it quite startling that a subject that was so under wraps, could be openly discussed in dramatisation by a Unit based in the War Office, and to be seen by the general public.

It made up the double-bill with *Where do we go from Here?* After the bomb indeed!

This part of the tour was presented by The Central Pool of Artists from December 3-21, 1945 playing eleven venues in the West Country, including Warminster, Exeter, Salisbury, Newton Abbott and Plymouth.

In Plymouth it was wonderful to play in the famous Globe Theatre in the Royal Marine Barracks. What a gem.

In Salisbury in the Arts Centre we were promoted as "Stars in Battledress", and reviewed as 'Two plays, as fast as a revue and as dramatic as a thriller'.

In *The Bomb's All Yours*, I doubled-up in the 27 different characters, as the English Scientist and the Anglican Bishop.

Both these plays were produced by Capt Andre Van Gyseghem.

***

As we opened the New Year in 1946, we gave a presentation that perhaps notably described the essential style of the ABCA Play Unit.

It was in the Kingsway Hall, London, on January 4th 1946, and billed as part of a Conference of Secondary School scholars on World Citizenship..

We arrived at the Hall the night before the performance complete with our lorry-load of equipment, only to find that the staging facilities were quite impossible for our set!

And that considering we'd played in just about every style of venue was surprising to say the least.

We were playing *Where Do We Go From Here?* which particularly needed special setting and complicated lighting.

Desperate! No alternative space was available.

The Conference, however, could not be disappointed Every seat had been booked and arrangements made to put extra chairs in the gangways. (Those were the days!)

Many ideas to solve the problems were proposed and all discarded. However, eventually, it was decided that the show would be attempted with no set at all.

No masked entrances or exits, nothing but the players, the lighting and a bare minimum of properties.

Thus, on the morning of Jan 4th 1946, if there had been a curtain at Kingsway Hall it would have gone up, for then the first spot struggled in the semi-darkness, and the performance began, with little or no visual help to charm the imaginations and create what was to become the most spontaneous burst of cheering and applause from hundreds of future "World Citizens".

The repeated curtain calls on that day (if there had been one) made us feel well-pleased and that truly the seal had been well set on work well-done by the Second Company of the ABCA Play Unit.

With the continuation of the war in Japan and the far east one more script was prepared called *The Japanese Way*. The title was self explanatory, and that came extra-mural to my involvement.

***

Out of that peculiar association of Actors in the Army in odd and unexpected endeavours, remain pleasing memories still.

I don't forget the Sergeant-Major of one RA Unit who greeting us said, he was 'so glad to see us because there was to be a General's inspection, and we'd help to take the gentleman's mind off his inspection of the Camp'.

Then there were the widely varying "Theatres" in which we played; from the modern and completely equipped as at Caerwent RN Factory, to the hall at HMS Glenholt where we played over the cookhouse, with the extra aromas thrown in (and what a grand audience it was!), and again the excellent "Globe Theatre" tucked away inside the Royal Marine barracks at Plymouth, and that compared with the vastness of the converted airplane hanger at Newtown.

Only once during all that time on the road, did we have to disappoint our audience when a performance had to be cancelled because the lorry carrying our equipment had a puncture, miles from our destination at Llanhilleth, South Wales. Our previous ingenuity didn't help then.

All crowned by the ringing cheers of those young people, tiers upon tiers of them, at the last performance in Kingsway Hall in London.

The truly motley crew of rich personalities in this Company of actor-soldiers (or soldier-actors) and backstage creators, where the stars were rightly only in the night sky, where the team meant everything in this still wartime environment.

Where actors and all were each his/her own stage-hand, electrician, props, odd-jobber and anything else that made the Company successful.

But changing times and that second company of the ABCA Play Unit then disappeared with demob and with reorganisation. Just one Company evolved into the Army Topical Theatre which then continued to please audiences in the Middle-East Command, with performances of the ABCA plays and highlighted by a special production of Shakespeare's *Othello* with Sergeant Alan Badel playing the lead.

In retrospect the period after VE Day for me, with the ABCA Play Unit, at the Central Pool of Artistes, was an extremely, very lucky, break. Having the opportunity while still in the Army to join full-time what was essentially a professional theatre company, with great talents, and then especially to be involved with the modern "Living Newspaper" type of production was a fine learning experience.

It provided a unique bridge from National Service back into civvy street after six years. I couldn't have wished for better.

Unplanned.

Lucky boy!

Certainly if I had planned it I'd have made a mess of it all.

Thus, after those six years my Soldier's Release Book was issued, dated 14th April 1946.

My Service Trade was described as 'Signal Instructor – Qualified, Distinguished'. "Any other qualification for civilian employment" – Actor. My Military Conduct was described as "Exemplary", and my Testimonial read:

'First-class soldier – an excellent organiser and administrator as Sergeant, he is a good leader and instructor and easily has the respect of his men. In his profession as an Actor he works well and enthusiastically, and should do very well.'

A charmed wartime.

At the time I was so thankful, but then as recollection takes over, I reflect on my living through those horrific years when the majority of young and old were giving up their lives, the supreme sacrifice, that my record has no battle medals, no service in foreign fields, just: 'As an Actor – should do well'.

I still wished I could have been an Airman and "done my bit"… Fate or whatever just decided otherwise.

So I left the Service with my War Gratuity (fourteen shillings per month) and Post War credits totalling £87, three shillings and six pence, and my demob suit.

I had chosen a grey herring-bone light-weight cloth.

It felt good…

Then, to set-up something like a real family with Margaret and baby Martin (now two years old) at, the top floor of 29 Wilberforce Road, Finsbury Park, London N4.

What now?

The real test.

Chapter Four

To be or not...?

What now indeed?

After six years of being "looked after" by HM Armed Services, it was a new experience again. It was now all up to me.

It was indeed a release, but was it going to be cold outside?

Having now spent some while treading the boards with the pros, and with the testimonial ringing in my ears, "Should do well", I could hardly consider the Shipping-clerk option as at all attractive.

My old CO Major Michael Macowan. who had taken me into the ABCA Play Unit was now back "in the biz" running the Arts Council of Great Britain, and he must surely be the person to contact. In charge of so many of the important civic theatres in the country he would tell me where all the jobs were available.

Full of enthusiasm I wrote to tell him that I was now demobbed.

High hopes.

Michael replied, asking me if I'd ever considered Stage-management?

Hopes dashed.

I was astonished that he did not apparently consider me an Actor!

It was cold outside.

Now the hard competitive 'biz' was revealed. Such a change from the camaraderie of the past years under stress we had experienced.

Hopes dashed, yes, but after the shock I soon resolved to prove my own intentions. I had taken a long time to test my acting capabilities before the War.

Not even attracted to that life at first. Only step by step and testing against others' assessments, did I get convinced of the possibilities I had.

At least enough to test myself now, and be confident enough, in the world of British Equity.

While I picked myself up and even before I'd decided on my next move, my unplanned life continued to open up.

Out of the blue I heard from my old friend of the Tavistock Rep. pre-war days, Leonard Crainford.

The last time I had heard was when he was running the CEMA office in the Midlands and I was in Alton Towers.

Now he was General Manager of the Festival Company at the Shakespeare Memorial Theatre at Stratford-upon-Avon, which was under the Direction of Sir Barry Jackson.

They were putting together the Company for the first season after the war (1946), and Leonard Crainford was offering me a contract for the 23-week season – 'to play as cast', opening on April 20th!

Whoopie!

What a break.

So my Army release papers were dated April 14 and I opened at Stratford-upon-Avon on April 20th!

They were preparing three productions to be ready to open in the first week.

The first, was *The Tempest* in which I was in the group covered in the programme as 'Nymphs, Reapers, Shapes and Mariners'. How many changes of costume I had I've no idea, but I'm sure I did not dress up as a Nymph.

The Company was:

Robert Harris	Valerie Taylor
Robert Vernon	Ruth Lodge
David King-Wood	Julian Somers
Hugh Griffith	Myles Eason
Paul Scofield	David O'Brien

James Raglan	Vernon Fortescue
Paul Stephenson	Dudley Jones
Patrick Ross	Duncan Ross
Christian Morrow	Anthony Groser
Nancy Nevinson	Muriel Davidson
Joy Parker	Jennifer Coverdale
John Harrison	Donald Sinden
Michael Rose	William Avenell
Anthony Hooper	Leonard White
David Hobman	Trevor Barker
June Monkhouse	Eileen Clark
Sulwen Morgan	Pamela Leatherland
Pat Brewer	Barbara Ormerod
Frances Brette	Robin Griffin

...described at that time as 'Probably the youngest ever to play at Stratford'.

The Tempest was produced by Eric Crozier.

Scenery and costumes designed by Paul Shelving.

Music composed by Lennox Berkeley.

Robert Harris played Prospero, Joy Parker was Miranda;

Ariel was played by the boy actor, David O'Brien.

Caliban was Julian Somers and Ferdinand by John Harrison.

Cymbeline opened next (April 23rd) and was of course the celebratory Birthday Play.

In this I got into a featured role, playing Caius Lucius, General of the Roman Forces.

Valerie Taylor, our leading lady, was introduced beautifully playing Imogen.

Paul Scofield playing Cloten in this season which proved him to be such a wonderful actor.

Production was by Nugent Monck, who was famous for running the Maddermarket Theatre in Norwich.

We had rehearsed to begin with in London, and I shall never forget one highlight in the rehearsal-room. We were coming to the first full run-through of the play and we awaited Mr Monck's 'Go!'.

Apprehension and quiet..

On the dot Mr Monck settled himself and addressed us:

'Ladies and Gentlemen, I want you to imagine that the audience are in – now get them out again as soon as possible.'

Again and again since then those words have echoed in my mind. What wonderful advice. No nonsense, no "milking it".

During the run – *Cymbeline* remained in repertory until September 27th – two more incidents occurred which are engraved in my memory.

Cymbeline – King of Britain was played by James Raglan, a fine "old stager".

Act 3 opens in a room in Cymbeline's Palace.

The King is playing host to Caius Lucius, the emissary from Julius Caesar.

In essence, Lucius has come to remind Britain that a tribute of some three-thousand pounds is a debt outstanding, and they'd better pay up.

Needless to say the King has no intention of doing so.

The stage is set for a banquet with a gathering at a long table and the room full of courtiers etc.

Up stage centre is the King and Lucius, guest of honour.

The King has several longish speeches to deliver.

On this particular occasion etched into my memory, Jimmy Raglan in full spate strangely goes into gibberish – he has dried! But he doesn't stop uttering noises that might just sound like Shakespeare... Gradually around the table everyone becomes aware that the speech is not the speech at all. Then everyone on stage realises.

Those seated at the table facing upstage are at pains trying to contain themselves, but Jimmy keeps it up relentlessly and is now adding flamboyant gestures to decorate the "performance".

It seemed to go on for some time, certainly long enough to demand a cue from prompt. But no cue came.

Whoever was on the book hadn't, seemingly, been aware of the usual signs of a dry. No uncomfortable pauses.

The dialogue was still going on.

At last, miraculously, without pausing, Jimmy surprisingly picked up his real lines again and continued as if nothing had happened.

The extraordinary thing about that was the fact that it all passed off without any of the usual awful reaction from the audience which happens when they sense an actor has dried.

That cold silence which shoots through the auditorium.

I really think that on that occasion the audience just thought that the acoustics at the Memorial Theatre were not all that good, and so they just leaned forward in their seats a little, to try to catch the lines.

But what a presence and confidence of the old actor, up to all the tricks, Jimmy was able to carry it off.

I was very impressed.

I've never forgotten it.

Of a very different kind, there was another experience in that same production which occurred to me, which illustrated just how inexperienced I was at that time as compared with Jimmy Raglan on stage. It has remained to haunt me.

'Act 4 Scene 2, An Exterior-Wales. Before a cave....' Previously a fight had taken place in which the character Cloten has been beheaded. (Strong, dramatic stuff). Later, all the audience are focused on a spotlit, filled sack lying in a clearing. Then, ENTER, Stage-left:

I, as Caius Lucius, full of importance, leading a Captain, other Officers and a Soothsayer.

On seeing the sack, I stop the group and say,

'Soft ho! What trunk is here without his top?'

There followed the most enormous spontaneous burst of laughter from the audience!

I was absolutely shocked. Totally thrown, I don't know how I got through the rest of that very serious scene.

I had no idea of how or why the audience thought it was funny. Especially THAT funny.

Was it something I said?

The way I said it?

Failure!

Whatever, eventually, I did learn a good lesson from that moment.

Remember to play comedy seriously. I never forgot.

But I was so scared stiff in playing that line on the second performance. I didn't know what to do with it. Thankfully, Valerie Taylor helped me back to my confidence, she was so wonderful and supportive. Urging me not to feel it so disastrous.

'It happens. It'll not happen again tonight,' she said.

And it didn't.

Many moons later the horror of that shock kept coming back to me. And I have reflected and wondered if perhaps Sir Barry Jackson was in that Birthday Night audience, and perhaps whether he downgraded me there and then?

I didn't get invited back for the 1947 season.

But, considering what did happen after that Stratford 1946 season (more anon), that was actually fortunate for me.

Cymbeline played for three performances in that first week, and then the third production in the season,

Love's Labours Lost opened on April 26th.

It was the notable production which shot Director, Peter Brook into the limelight.

He received an ovation on the first night for 'brilliant handling of a difficult play.'

In this I was again in the cluster of Lords, Heralds and Rustics.

But watching the work of Peter Brook with David King-Wood as Berowne, Valerie Taylor as Princess of France, Paul Scofield as Don Armado, Hugh Griffith as Holofernes, it was so worthwhile just to be around.

I did have to take particular interest in *Love's Labours Lost* throughout the run, because some time later in the season it was realised that there were no understudies in place. Hastily rehearsals were called and I was given Berowne to understudy. I was never called upon however, and indeed never had more than one rehearsal. On that account I was glad not to be called, because I was hardly right for or indeed experienced enough for such a role.

The programme for this play carried a most unusual announcement:

'The loud-speaking equipment in this Theatre is the first of its kind to be used. It was designed and installed by Decca Radio and Television.'

So there!

The audience having difficulty with James Raglan's gibberish in *Cymbeline* might indeed have had some effect to improve the acoustics. Who knows?

Henry V was introduced into the repertory on May 10th.

In that I doubled as Lord Scroop and the Duke of Orleans. Two baddies for the price of one.

There was quite a lot of "doubling" in this production.

With forty-three roles to cast this was inevitable.

Indeed, Douglas Seale who had now joined the Company played three roles (Bardolph, Sir Thomas Erpingham, and a French Soldier).

Among the Lords and Ladies were three new names, Duncan Goddard, Lyndon Mason and Richard Renny.

Paul Scofield was truly fine as the King, adding to his laurels for the season. I was full of admiration. If only I could aspire to his excellence.

The play was produced by Dorothy Green.

In the sixth week, *As You Like It* was introduced on May 31st. That was produced by Herbert M Prentice (by permission of Sheffield Repertory Company Ltd).

In this, Orlando was played by Myles Eason, Oliver by Paul Scofield, Rosalind by Ruth Lodge, Celia by Joy Parker, Jacques by Julian Somers, and Touchstone by Hugh Griffith.

I played the First Lord – attending on the banished Duke.

By this time the joy of playing at Stratford-upon-Avon for that first season after the War, was enhanced wonderfully by Margaret and our young Martin (now two years old) coming to stay with me in the town. We enjoyed a lovely summer living in Limes Avenue.

We weren't the only parents to have a young baby in the Company. Paul Scofield and Joy Parker also had a young boy, the same age and by chance also the same name, Martin. It became quite a feature around town to see both Joy and Margaret with their respective young lads on the backs of their bikes riding about.

Indeed over fifty years later, Paul wrote on a postcard to us:

'I still see you, Margaret, in my memory's eye, cycling through Stratford with your Martin either on the front or the back of your bike, what a lovely time that was.' (January 23rd, 1999).

I don't know what started me off but during that summer I began to try my hand at sketching portraits of other members of the Company. My efforts, though I thought them very ordinary, did seem to attract some interest.

Surprisingly a small exhibition was mounted in the Hathaway Café.

Some actually sold!

I did one of Valerie Taylor which she liked and which inspired her to do one of me!

A nice keepsake which I cherish still.

By the ninth week of the season, six different productions could be seen in the same week. *Macbeth* was added on June 22nd. I played Angus.

Michael Macowan joined the Company to produce, and considering that only a few months previously on my demob Michael had written me suggesting that I might take up stage-management, I think he was surprised to find me acting in the Company at Stratford.

However I have to say that he was entirely magnanimous in accepting that he may have mis-judged me earlier.

Indeed so much so that a few years later (1951) he had me cast as one of four who made up the characters for the premiere of Christopher Fry's play, *A Sleep of Prisoners*, which he directed.

I will re-live that wonderful opportunity later...

However, in the *Macbeth* (1946) Robert Harris played the lead and Valerie Taylor played the Lady. Banquo was David King-Wood, Macduff being Julian Somers, Paul Scofield played Malcolm.

The next play to be introduced was the only non-Shakespeare; Marlowe's *The Tragical History of Dr Faustus*, produced by Walter Hudd.

It opened on July 13th

Robert Harris was Faustus, Hugh Griffith, Mephistophilis.

I was the Bad Angel and John Harrison, The Good Angel (I hope those were not casting to type!).

Helen of Troy was Jennifer Coverdale (as "the face that launched a thousand ships" that certainly could have been casting to type!).

Two more names joined the Company at this time in the Lords, Ladies, Attendants, Monks, Friars and Devils departments – Maxwell Jackson and Herbert Roland.

Herbert Roland went on to become a long-standing friend and later on a successful Television Director with CBC in Toronto.

The repertory for Stratford 1946 was completed when *Measure for Measure* opened on August 23rd. This made it possible for all eight plays to be seen in weeks 19, 22 and the final week 23.

This last production only had nine performances in that season, but I believe that it was due to be seen again in the next season. It was my play out.

I've wondered since if it had already been decided that I would not be re-called for 1947 and therefore not cast in this last play? But probably my surmise is quite unfounded as some of those who were cast were also not recalled like myself.

Measure for Measure was notable in that Frank McMullan was brought over from the USA (Yale University) to do this production. I wish that I could have worked with him. But I did have a chance to work with an American director, – Norris Houghton- later on.

Overall, this season at the Memorial Theatre, Stratford upon Avon was a wonderful re-introduction to civvy street after those six long years in the Army.

Although my roles were only supporting (or less) they did achieve some attention.

I was surprised, indeed, to find I had a small following at the stage-door, and in the mail. That was a new experience…

But working with such fine talents as Robert Harris, Valerie Taylor, Paul Scofield and the rest of that Company which included the early days of such important names as, Donald Sinden, John Harrison, Hugh Griffith, Nancy Nevinson, Duncan Ross, Dudley Jones, Douglas Seale, Julian Somers, Peter Brook and more, was training rare and of high order.

My first pro salary was £8 per week.

Ruth Ellis (*Stratford-upon-Avon Herald*), writing her overview of the season included: 'It would be agreeable to dwell on many smaller parts, but among the voices we hope to hear again are Leonard White's…' and in a personal letter to me she wrote: 'I liked your work very much indeed, and hope to see more of it. The Bad Angel in particular had real character and power.'

In fact, that particular role led to my next job immediately after Stratford. As it happened, the famous actor, Baliol Holloway saw me play The Bad Angel in *Dr Faustus*, and was instrumental in getting me cast as Oberon in the production of *A Midsummer Night's Dream*, which he was co-producing (with John Counsell) at the Theatre Royal, Windsor.

So I didn't get recalled for the 1947 season at Stratford but I did continue immediately with a step-up in my Shakespeare roles, and with a splendid cast.

Mary Kerridge played Titania, with Bruno Barnabe, Malcolm Russell, John Witty, Peter Rosser, Rule Pyott, Hugh Cruttwell, Arnold Pilbeam, George Hurst, Stanford Holme, George S Wray, Sheila Bellamy, Jennifer Gray, Rosaline Haddon, Stuart Burge, Jean Raley, Pauline Renton, Margaret Balfrey, Henrietta Edwards, and of course the superb Baliol Holloway playing "his" role of Bottom.

In the true repertory style of that time (we opened October 15th, 1946) several of the actors were also on the "Executive staff" of the Theatre. The Manager was Arnold Pilbeam, the Associate Producer was Stanford Holme, the Assistant Manager, Hedley Mattingley, the Stage Director, Hugh Cruttwell (who later became Head of RADA so successfully).

A wonderful team under John Counsell.

I enjoyed Oberon.

And this meant of course that I was back in London again and available after Oberon.

Testing the routine of visits to the Labour Exchange and trying to establish an Agent and hoping....

Finsbury Park was not exactly as attractive as Stratford-upon Avon, but it did provide easy access to the West End theatre world. A necessary address.

And we still could take advantage of trips back to the seaside at Newhaven, as well as occasional visits to Wellington in Somerset where Margaret still had family ties, and happy memories of many of her own young holidays with Auntie Wyn.

All good for young Martin, now three years old, to get away from the "smoke".

The facility (and luck) with which I had moved from demob into professional theatre, meant that I had gone back on my word given to Margaret before the war that I wouldn't be a professional actor. I was very fortunate in that she never complained, and never reminded me of my promise.

But, now was the testing time, after a long engagement.

The term "resting" came to have its different meaning.

***

It was 1947. I managed to introduce myself to BBC Radio, with engagements for BBC Schools. I think the first was in a series called *Off the Syllabus* in which I was the Narrator for a programme *An Episode of the Terror*, a radio play based on the story of Balzac, by Sam Langdon (Feb 11, 1947).

Unfortunately, this same month my old Headmaster and Mentor-extraordinary, (at Meeching School, Newhaven) died.

Apart from his great encouragement in the Arts he had during his life, used his influence to make sure that youngsters carried responsibility in the local Christ Church, while still at school. He got young Richard Beal and me appointed as Sidesmen.

That role had not before been carried by schoolboys.

Alas, I was not able to attend Ernest James Coker's funeral as I was playing a matinee performance in Brighton's Theatre Royal.

Yes, I'd had the good fortune to join a new company called Duchess Plays Ltd whose Artistic Directors were Robert Helpmann and Michael Benthall.

Their first production was a revival of the 1612 play, John Webster's *The White Devil*.

Robert Helpmann played the lead, Flamineo, and the rest of the fine Company were Margaret Rawlings, Roderick Lovell, Martita Hunt, Andrew Cruikshank, Hugh Griffith, Wolfe Morris, Mayura, Joan Schofield, Gordon Davies, Stanley Radcliffe, Norman Webb, John Benson, John Toray, Edgar Whitburn, Anthony Bridges, Thelma Ruby, Joan Drant. Also this cast introduced two young wonderful talents, in Heather Stannard and Claire Bloom.

The *Avenger* (much later) Patrick Macnee, spoke one line in that play, and attracted critical approval from Harold Hobson (*Sunday Times* March 19, 1947).

I played Count Lodovico. (My West-end debut, was £10, five shillings per week of eight performances).

We opened pre-London, at the Theatre Royal in Brighton on February 17th, 1947.

It was good to have a week back in Sussex and to be able to stay in the old home again.

After opening night, I was called to see Michael Benthall and Robert Helpmann and told that a scene which had been cut from the play, was to be reinstated.

This meant that I was to open the play in which the enraged Lodovico storms on to the stage shouting 'Banished!'

Quite fitting to set the scene for all the blood and thunder to follow.

I was elated.

The next week we were in Nottingham at another Theatre Royal.

It was a viciously cold winter, and we were still suffering the restrictions of the wartime (if not worse).

The dressing-rooms were like ice-wells.

Fortunately the Webster "poetry and passion" warmed us up, and I hope – the audience as well.

We followed the pantomime at that theatre.

Slapstick to mayhem.

The Nottingham Guardian's critic, headed it 'High Drama at the Royal'. Powerful acting… in a production that throughout was finely staged and dressed…

I was included in those credited as 'uniformly high talented'.

Then we opened at the Duchess Theatre in London on March 6th, 1947. A small theatre for a big drama.

It was reviewed twice in the *Sunday Times*.

The first-night by Harold Hobson and later by James Agate in his *Catching-Up* column.

Hobson wrote: 'Mr Benthall punctuates his production with stabs and flashes of electricity. But what we get in fullest measure is not lightning but lightning's slower brother, thunder… A couple of assassins, isolated by a lurid shaft of limelight on a darkened stage begin the performance with a tremendous clatter and din…'

I was one of the assassins!

'The performance thus has to be tuned to a perpetual climax… Then treading on silence, a page quietly says these five words, "This is not true Madam". That is all. As this play counts noise, it is hardly more than a whisper. Yet for me it was the most striking moment…'

Those five words were spoken by Patrick Macnee.

Six years later, I was casting Patrick to play Corporal Adams in Christopher Fry's wonderful play *A Sleep of Prisoners* for its Canadian premiere in Toronto. And then in another seven years afterwards, for his John Steed role in ABC-TV's *The Avengers*.

But, back to *The White Devil*, in 1947. James Agate summed it up with 'I congratulate the entire company… To the reader whose only interest in criticism is the answer to the question "Shall I enjoy this play?" my answer is simple. If you get a pleasurable shudder at lines like "Millions now in their graves, which at last day like mandrakes shall rise shrieking," you will. If you think the Last Trump should sound to the strain of *Oh, What a Beautiful Morning*, you won't.'

WA Darlington (*Daily Telegraph*) although finding it an 'exciting production', was not so fond of the play.

'What a tangle *The White Devil* makes of a straightforward story.' But he praises Martita Hunt ('A lovely piece of acting') and Robert Helpmann, who 'dripped villainy'. Margaret Rawlings, Andrew Cruikshank and Roderick Lovell also 'did admirable work'.

Critic Ivor Brown, wrote: 'It is a brave venture to do this kind of play unsubsidised in the heart of the commercial theatres of the West-End'.

One particular incident sticks in my memory.

I used to make a habit of getting to stand in the wings early for the curtain-call, so that I could watch Robert Helpmann play his last scene, his death scene, which Webster makes to go on seemingly for ever.

In the action, just prior to Flamineo having been left for dying, a lantern which he had been carrying had been knocked out of his hand and lies on the ground.

The stage is dark except for the spotlight on him.

But, on this particular occasion the lantern which normally went out, remained dimly lit, flickering on and off.

Each time it went off I thought it would stay off, but it didn't. It kept, it seemed, struggling to stay alight throughout Flamineo's long farewell.

As he found new strength to keep alive, so the light in the lamp found new energy.

But at last, the long last, as he came to the end of his life, the lamp went out, and it stayed out! As if on cue.

A truly magical moment, I couldn't believe my eyes.

That audience had seen a unique performance.

It never happened again of course. True theatre...

And that reminds me of another unique theatre experience which was even more impressive.

We – Margaret with me – were at Oberammergau for the Passion Play in 1970.

Above: My father, Thomas George White and mother, Maria Rebecca White (nee Tasker) in mid-life, before I surprised them…

Right: Three Sisters – Susan (Nance) pram right; pram left Eva; Alice in pram.

Father – Jack of all trades. More interested in the horses than the laundry.

Above: 1916. My first entrance – and I knew where the camera was!

Below: Margaret as a young girl, with her baby brother, Roger.

Top: Introducing my new sister, Mary.

Above: My brother Tom, probably taken about the time I was born (1916).

Below: My father and Golden Cup.

My father's first paper-shop in Newhaven. This was a publicity stunt to launch the new Sunday paper, the Sunday Graphic. In the doorway is my older brother; behind him is my sister, Alice. I am in the soapbox on wheels (age 10). My young sister, Mary, is hiding her face - she has Mumps. My father is on the right.

My first bike, in the back yard at Brooklyn.

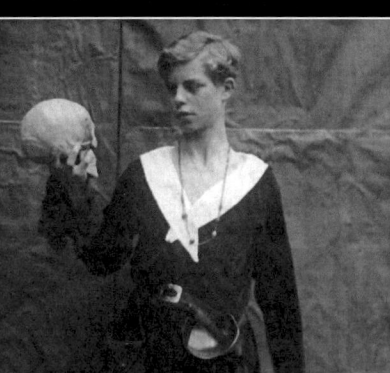

Left top and middle: School play, 1930, playing Queen Gertrude in *Hamlet*, with Norman Elderkin as Claudius and Leslie Clark in the title role.

Brutus in *Julius Caesar* (1934/35).

Below: School play: King Richard I (1934/35), including me as the Queen

Above: On the Meeching School Committee, second left, back row.

Right: Summer Games. Younger sister Mary and I join some of the family cricket team (Meeching Down).

Tavistock Repertory Company, London:

Left: General von Gadenau in *Miracle at Verdun*, 1938.

Tavistock Repertory Company, London:
As The Captain with Edith Rose in
Shaw's *Androcles and the Lion* (1939).

Above, left: Panto – *Dick Whittington* – Demon Rat (R) Stage Left, 1939.

Above, right: The Tavistock Rep Company leaving London for their Tour of Wales (1939).

Left: Margaret Kent, on holiday in Bognor Regis c, 1937. I cycled 20 miles to take this photo!

As Dr Harry Trench with Martin Benson, Margaret Godwin, Wilfred Sultan and Rowland F White, in *Widowers' Houses* (Shaw), 1939.

Above: Compassionate leave – winter wedding at St Stephen's Church Hounslow Feb 28, 1942. (L-R, Father, Mother, sister Alice, Margaret's father, Me – Cpl White (Signals), Margaret's mother, Margaret (nee Kent), Joan Rogers (Margaret's cousin), Grannie Kent.

Left: A new role – called-up to the Royal Berkshire Regt.

Our first son, Martin Guy, born 1944.

Left: Martin Guy – 'A posy for Mum'.

Below: Our second son. Stephen Grant (born 1949, City of London Hospital) – here thinking of Art College?

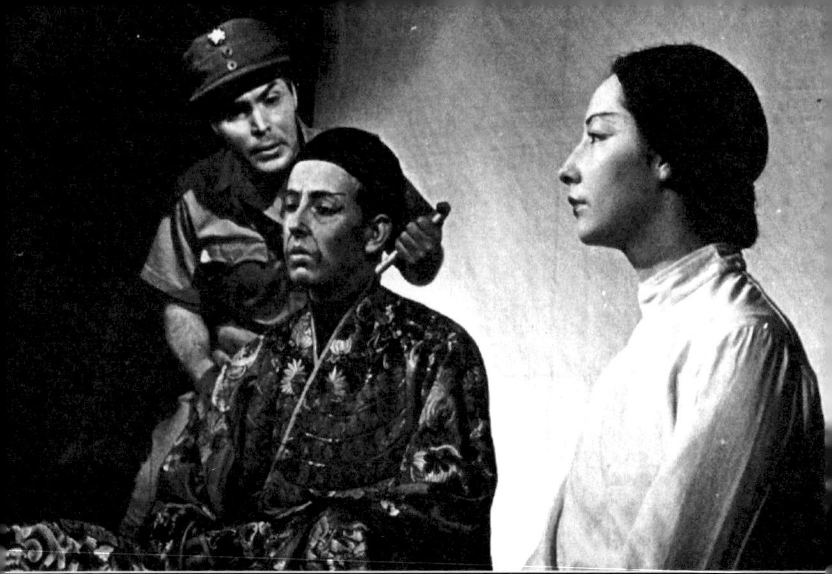

ABCA (Army Bureau of Current Affairs) Play Unit
Above: The Great Swap (Ted Willis and Jack Lindsay, 1945) as Chinese Office
(with Geoffrey Colville and Enid Drummond Young)

The Greek Man
(with Enid Drummond Young)

Above: Memorial Theatre, Stratford-upon-Avon, 1946. As Lord Scroop in *Henry V.*

Below: Cymbeline, Stratford-upon-Avon, 1946, as Cauis Lucius.

Above: ABCA Play Unit. As Member of Parliament in *Where Do We Go From Here* (Boland and Willis), 1945.

Arts Council (GB) Midland Theatre
Company. Coventry: *Musical Chairs*
(1949). As Joseph Schindler
with Joy Harvey.
Below: With Benedicta Leigh.

A Month in the Country (Turgenev), as Rakitin with Joy Harvey, 1949.

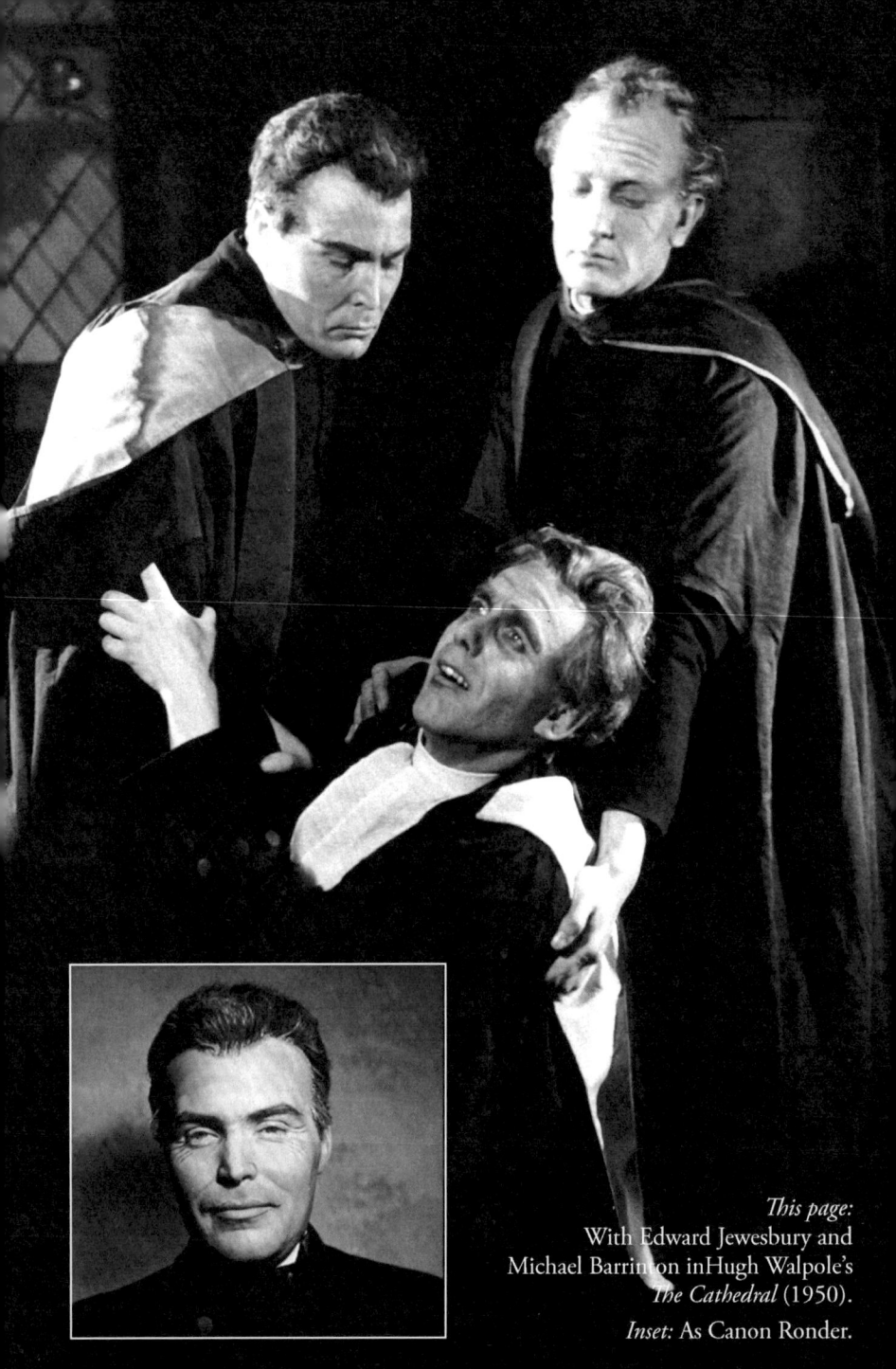

An early film for Independent Artists:
The Dark Man – playing Detective
Evans with Edward Underdown (1951).

He Who Gets Slapped (Andreyev/Guthrie), Duchess Theatre, 1947. As Bezano with *Right:* Audrey Fildes and *Below:* Robert Helpmann.

Off stage

Point of Departure (Anouilh/Kitty Black Tennant Productions Ltd), 1950-51

Above: Mathias, with Mai Zetterling

This page: London, 1951-52. Christopher Fry's Festival of Britain premiere, *A Sleep of Prisoners.* As David King, with Denholm Elliott, Stanley Baker and Hugh Pryse.

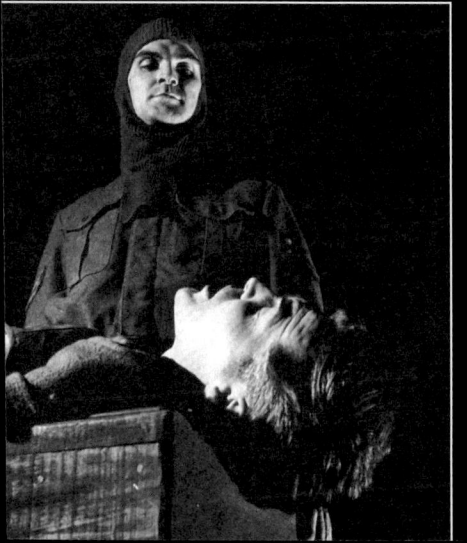

A Sleep of Prisoners New York premiere introducing Donald Harron (taking over from Denholm Elliott).

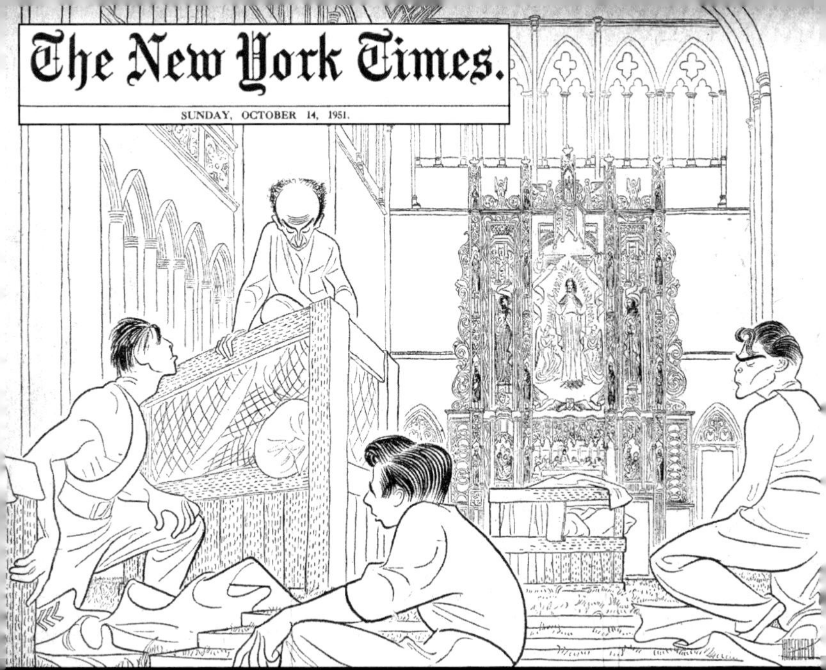
The New York Times.
SUNDAY, OCTOBER 14, 1951.

Above:

A Sleep of Prisoners - Hirschfield drawing, *New York Times*, Sunday October 14, 1951. Stanley Baker, Hugh Pryse, Donald Harron and me.

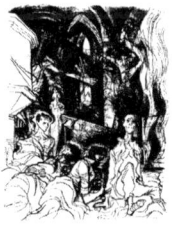

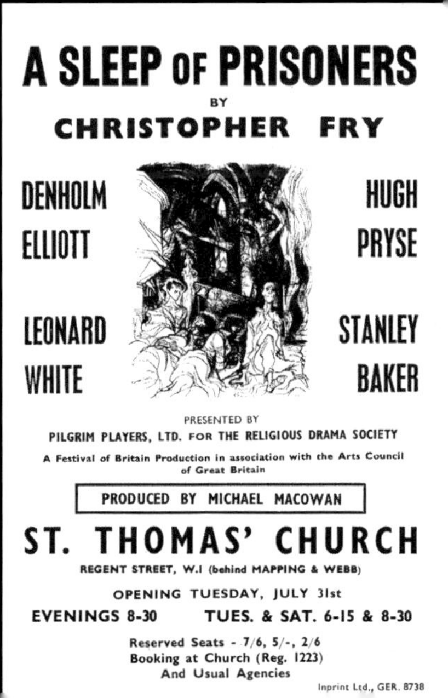
A SLEEP OF PRISONERS
BY
CHRISTOPHER FRY
DENHOLM ELLIOTT
HUGH PRYSE
LEONARD WHITE
STANLEY BAKER
PRESENTED BY
PILGRIM PLAYERS, LTD. FOR THE RELIGIOUS DRAMA SOCIETY
A Festival of Britain Production in association with the Arts Council of Great Britain
PRODUCED BY MICHAEL MACOWAN
ST. THOMAS' CHURCH
REGENT STREET, W.1 (behind MAPPING & WEBB)
OPENING TUESDAY, JULY 31st
EVENINGS 8-30
TUES. & SAT. 6-15 & 8-30
Reserved Seats - 7/6, 5/-, 2/6
Booking at Church (Reg. 1223)
And Usual Agencies
Inprint Ltd., GER. 8738

Right:

A Sleep of Prisoners - handbill with Ronald Searle caricatures

Reception in Chicago (Evanston):

Left to right: Me, Ruth Cugat, Stanley Baker, Lucille Lortel (Producer), Clarence Derwent (taking over from Hugh Pryse), Ellen Baker, Donald Harron.

I was entirely impressed by the whole event and the magnificence of the staging, but on that occasion, the production had come to the moment when Christ is to be nailed to the Cross.

The hammer was raised and struck the first blow, and then absolutely as though on cue, an enormous crash of thunder cracked down from the hills behind the open-air amphitheatre, followed by forked-lightning as though striking the Cross itself.

Phew! That was something. Chilling.

The vast audience stilled... Nature taking part.

No stage-manager could have created that effect.

***

But, again, returning to 1947, and the Duchess Theatre. It was great that Duchess Plays had the guts to launch that season, and I thank my lucky stars that this Company under Helpmann and Benthall and next, joined by the great Tony Guthrie, gave me the opportunity to be part of it.

After my run of Shakespeare, a touch of Marlowe, followed by Webster, and then into the Russian playwright, Leonid Andreyev, all providing a rare continuity for a young actor.

A high and rich standard.

He Who Gets Slapped opened on June 17th 1947, continuing that special season at the Duchess Theatre.

The English version of the Andreyev play was by Judith Guthrie, Tyrone Guthrie's wife.

I got a rise of nearly two pounds a week for this.

Coincidentally, that date was the anniversary of my first meeting with Margaret (in 1938), our "Red Rise Day".

So, it was specially auspicious.

I have two vibrant memories of rehearsals with Guthrie.

I was playing Bezano (the equestrian trainer in the circus), and Tony wanted to experiment with several different possible speech accents for the role.

He would suggest one and let me go with it for some time, and then just when I was getting settled with it, he would suggest another. This went on for some time. He particularly was not going to settle for a "stage Russian" (he was so right), and many different experiments just kept going on.

Eventually, I was getting worried thinking we were getting a bit too close to the opening for my comfort.

Whereas, I was getting nervy, Tony remained entirely calm and confident. He kept the rehearsal alive and fresh.

Then, after all, he decided to do – what I believe he wanted to do in the first place – to avoid the phoney "foreign" accents, and rely on the variations in our own natural voices to characterise the mix of a circus in the 1920s.

Then another surprise. On the day before opening, after the dress-rehearsal, Tony didn't think that my riding boots were "right". Instead of doing what most conventional directors would do and get the wardrobe mistress to sort it out, he decided to come with me and walk me around umpteen theatrical shoe-hire shops in Soho until he found a pair of boots that satisfied him.

I was amazed. At that highly critical time, when time was of the essence, and there must have been many more important things and people to deal with, he chose to concentrate on a detail, such as my riding boots!

I knew that Tony was expert and well-known for the big scene, the spectacular, and I was in awe, but here I discovered, and was so respectful of his fine attention to the detail. I knew he was great, but after working with him, I had found the Master.

It was working with a wonderful cast:

Robert Helpmann playing Prince (or the He of the title), Ernest Milton (Mancini), Audrey Fildes (Consuela), Margaret Diamond – (Zinaida – French actress, Suzy Prim was originally cast in this role, but Margaret Diamond took over before we opened).

Alfie Bass (who was Tilly), Erich Pohlmann (Baron Regnard), Peter Varley (Polly), Arnold Marle (Papa Briquet), Stanley Radcliffe (Jackson), Basil Coleman (A Gentleman), and I was Bezano. I was proud as it was the first time my name was printed in bold type in the cast-list in the programme.

Others in the big cast were:

Wolfe Morris	Anthony van Bridge
John Fitzgerald	Dinah Malone
Thelma Ruby	Claire Bloom
Winifred Hill	Matt Bell
William H Gainsford	Edgar Whitburn
Miriam Pritchett	Courtney Hume

and Tommy Frewer, all playing the Artistes of the circus.

I notice, as I read the programme all these moons later, that a famous name turns up as the Assistant Stage Manager – Lydia Kyasht Jnr – daughter of the famous Ballerina and teacher. Probably the nearest I ever got to the biz being glamorous! Young Lydia also later became a dramatist.

The first night of *He Who Gets Slapped* was not the best, alas. Very sadly, probably the most experienced actor, and most renowned in the cast, Ernest Milton, ran into trouble and needed the prompter.

Robert Helpmann marvellously rescued him and managed to take over Milton's lines that were essential to take the plot on, but unfortunately it was, to say the least, noticeable.

The reviews, however, were kind in that respect, and noted that Ernest Milton recovered well. Indeed the second night he was back on form and splendid.

'Mr Ernest Milton has caught the rhythm and the music of the foolish Count Mancini, and no doubt the words will come later.' (*Sunday Times*, June 22, 1947.)

'Robert Helpmann in the title role, playing his first prose part, as the prince who wants to be a clown, Margaret Diamond as a lion-tamer and Arnold Marle as the circus proprietor, are admirable, but it is Audrey Fildes as the guileless beauty with a cockney accent who steals this lovely show.' (Elspeth Grant, *D. Graphic* June 18, 1947.)

I did get a mention in *The Stage*:

'Leonard White's Bezano (Consuela's ring partner and lover) is robustly done.'

Angus McBean, the first-rate photographer, made a fine picture of Audrey and me in our roles, which I greatly cherish.

I have always been very surprised that Audrey did not continue her so successful career. She just seemed to vanish from the scene. Indeed many many moons later I found her in Canada seemingly having left the 'biz. A fine actress that I wished would have gone on to enhance our stages.

That 1947 season in London's West End was followed by my first attempt to "get into pictures".

I'd grown-up on my weekly visits to the local kinema when a school-boy, but old-enough to accompany and look after, my young sister Mary. In the days when a shilling (five new pennies after the Euro devaluation), would buy two seats in the "five-pennies" (and they were NOT in the cheap seats!) and have one penny change each to buy gobstoppers.

It so happens that Clifford Evans, film-star of that time, and who had been in the Army Bureau of Current Affairs, Play Unit with me; (I was his Sergeant, and I had obtained his release papers early so that he might be demobbed, before his time, to start to make a new movie) was later, when I was also back in civvy street, and he was about to start on yet another picture: he then, alerted me and got me a few days work on the film as a "directed extra".

That film was *The Silver Darlings*.

Clifford was co-starring with Helen Shingler, and also acting as Associate Director with Clarence Elder. It was a Holyrood Film Production made at Welwyn Garden City studios. One factory there making British films and next door the other factory making American Shredded Wheat.

The food production lasted longest.

I had just one scene as a Stornoway Fisherman, non-speaking thankfully. Me trying a Stornoway accent would not have pleased the good folk of Lewis.

I'm not sure how Clifford Evans got away with it as he was dyed-in-the-wool Welsh!

However it gave me some experience before the camera, and a chance to see what goes on in a film studio.

Clifford certainly taught me one lesson worth remembering.

It was almost the end of my one day and the last set-up. A pub scene. I was standing next to Clifford at the bar, while the shot was being lined-up. After a few minutes and just before the camera was to turn, Clifford quietly said to me, 'Stand closer'.

I moved closer to the bar.

'No. Closer to me.'

I thought I was standing quite naturally, well enough, but I moved a little towards him.

'No, up tight, quickly.'

I thought that a bit strange, but after a beat I did so.

The camera rolled, 'Take 1'.

After that take, the bell went for the wrap for the day.

Clifford then explained.

He said, as we walked away. 'By standing that close to me you had to be included in the shot and that means they have to call you again tomorrow!'

Ah! He had made sure that I had another day's pay.

Little tricks like that were worth knowing.

There was much to learn.

Distinctly different from theatre. And different again from the television camera in those early days.

'Hit your marks!'

'Stop face-acting!'...

Many moons later at some Festival in London I went to see that picture, *The Silver Darlings*.

I sat at the back. A habit I made later on many occasions. It was easier to escape without being seen.

The picture ran for ages, and I thought that perhaps I'd been left on the cutting-room floor? Another habit of the industry.

I'd just about given up, when, yes, the scene showed up. I didn't recognise myself! I couldn't believe it was me. I'd forgotten what I looked like in those many moons past.....Was it really me?

Anyway I'd made my screen debut proper.

Well, sort of...

***

I've tried to keep some chronological order in this, but the present keeps crashing through and making me pause,

A few years ago, for example, I picked up the morning paper and turned to the Obituary pages (that now has, also, become a habit, alas) and there looking at me was a photo of Christopher Fry... Oh, so, so sad.

He had represented, been responsible for I might say, the most important part of my acting career. Notably in 1951 and after, for several years.

The cord was broken.

Then again, the day after, the same routine, and I saw that actor James Doohan had died in the USA. He, noted for ever, seemingly, as Scotty in *Star Trek*. But my memory flashed back to him in earlier times, playing another Scot, for me, when I was directing Lister Sinclair's play *The Blood is Strong* for Jupiter Theatre, in Toronto in the early fifties....

Death won't wait.

But now, back in the late 'forties, and after my cinema/film debut, I picked up some radio work.

The BBC Home Service were making a series called *The Adventures of Captain Kettle*, produced by Charles Maxwell.

I was in several episodes, but my scrap-book doesn't mention if I had a name part, or was it just a voice as necessary? Probably just a voice.

It was fun to do. I liked radio. We recorded it with an audience in the old Paris Cinema studio in Lower Regent Street in London.

At this time, things were still overhanging from the War years. Rationing was, if anything, now worse, but the adventure of Peace, invigorating.

It was a time when several Sunday night theatre clubs existed to produce showcase performances in the West End. I was a member of Reunion Theatre Association – the title spoke for itself – which was a considerable help to many getting back into the Stage-doors.

Another was a group called The London Players Guild (patrons Flora Robson and Emlyn Williams) which "existed for the most laudable purpose of giving players unknown to London a chance to be seen".

I was in one of their productions at the Whitehall Theatre (Sunday night, October 12th, 1947).

It was an adaptation of Margaret Irwin's novel, *Still She Wished for Company* in which I played Lucien, Lord Chidleigh. Helen Lowry directed, and the cast included, Anne Stapledon, Maurice Browning, Patrick Ross, Rita Staines, Aimee Delamain, Derek Ensor and Theodore Meade.

Joan Riley did the lighting. Monica Stutfield was in charge of music. All, as it were, "on appro".

WA Darlington in the *Telegraph* thought the play had been showcased well: '..is worth serious consideration for a more elaborate production and a proper run.' But he was not so happy with the performances. I was only described as 'adequate'. What a damning word that is.

The review in the *Stage* newspaper however, was kinder,

'As Lord Chidleigh, Leonard White had the right air of romantic flamboyance and brought home the tragedy of frustration.'

During the short time I was in that theatre, which was running one of its successful farces, I noted that the Stage-Manager's "book" for the current play running, was in the prompt-corner. I nosed through it and was intrigued to discover that each performance had been recorded with the number of laughs achieved. I understood that if a certain number was not achieved at any time a post-mortem would be held!

You can't mess about with farce.

I can't believe that the Sunday night performance of mine had anything to do with my next break. Much more likely my work earlier at the Duchess Theatre in *The White Devil* or *He Who Gets Slapped* was responsible.

Whatever, I had the good fortune – after I gather a lot of candidates had been considered for the role – to get the part of Malcolm in Michael Redgrave's *Macbeth*.

It was a double bonus. Not only to work with Redgrave but also with the American Director, Norris Houghton.

We opened at the Royal Court Theatre in Liverpool on November 10th, 1947. A great cast:

Ena Burrell (Lady Macbeth), Michael Goodliffe, (Banquo), Clement McCallin (Macduff), Hector MacGregor (Ross).

With John Blatchley, Elizabeth Kentish, Paul Hansard, Douglas Wilmer, William Marsh, Roger Braban, Leslie Sands, Alan Hood, Donald Bain, Janet Joye, Richard Bebb-Williams, Keith Lloyd, Paddy Green, Gillian Webb, Oliver Ford, Clement Ashby, Wilfred Carter, Paul Hardwick, Stephen Darlot, Peter Bartlett, Lesley Merritt, Margot van der Burgh, Michael O'Halloran.

Design was by Paul Sheriff, music by Alan Bush.

It was a Tennant Productions Ltd presentation.

It was an unusual staging of the play insofar that the three witches (the weird sisters) were accompanied by their three masters, the warlocks, and it was well reviewed…

'Last night's premier production was so strikingly staged and acted, so rich in colour, and so grim and ghostly in its evocation of the supernatural that the sense of nightmare lingered even after the players had said their farewells…

'There is so much talent in the Company and Norris Houghton's production, is of such outstanding quality, that as it was played last night, will be one of the lasting memories of a lifetime.' (AMA – *Liverpool Daily Post*)

'A magnificently staged and finely acted *Macbeth* won a tremendous ovation at the Royal Court Theatre, Liverpool, last night' (*Daily Mail*).

'I cannot recommend it too highly; anyone interested in the theatre generally, and in Shakespeare particularly, should not miss this production (*Evening Express*).'

We then moved on to the Grand Theatre in Blackpool and again garnered excellent reviews.

'*Macbeth* is an Everest that has tested the mettle of many great players. but up the Shakespearean slopes, Mr Redgrave and his gallant company climb to an impressive height' (*BB Evening Gazette*).

We did some schools' matinees, and in Blackpool one such performance provoked a news report in the *West Lancashire Evening Gazette* – 'New Crown for Macbeth'

Nearly 1700 Blackpool school children gave Shakespeare and Michael Redgrave the reception of their distinguished careers at the Grand Theatre yesterday afternoon. Out of the classical dust of the schoolroom, Macbeth, with all its pageantry, drama and colour, burst upon their young minds with medieval grandeur. They adored the three witches, hissed the murderers, shouted with excitement at the murder of Lady Macduff, and made the rafters ring over the clash of arms.

But there was one item they were totally unprepared for. When Macbeth kissed Lady Macbeth with some degree of emotional warmth, they laughed, cheered, whistled.

They were delighted that Shakespeare could be so human. Mr Redgrave and Miss Ena Burrill as Lady Macbeth had some difficulty in concealing their own amusement!

At curtainfall, the youngsters loudly demanded Macbeth's presence.

In his speech, Mr Redgrave noted that when he was kissing Lady Macbeth her locks had become entangled in his sleeve, and had required a certain amount of extricating.

He hoped if they had to write essays, the incident would be left out. He told them they had been a marvellous audience.

Outside the theatre they blocked the street chanting 'We want Michael Redgrave...' and for nearly half-an-hour he was kept busy signing autograph books.

'They were terrific', he said...'

However, one incident in that performance was not recorded.

At one point we were aware of strange pinging noises around us on stage, but soon to discover that the noises were made by pea-shooters being fired at us!

It went on for a little while, until Michael Redgrave took charge, stopped acting, and walked down to the footlights, and launched into a headmaster-like telling off, reminding them of how they ought to behave…

The result, loud applause from the rest (who hadn't got pea-shooters, and probably some who wished that they had) and Michael resumed his performance.

The next week we were in Glasgow, at the vast Theatre Royal, where if you stand on the stage you can only just about see the back of the Gallery. It was part of the routine in those days when touring to get to the theatre on the Monday morning, check at the stage-door for any mail, see if the laundry had come, check the dressing-room allocation (and if first, bag the best make-up mirror and make sure all the lights worked) but most importantly just to walk on to the stage and assess the auditorium.

Here, as I noted the overall size and the distance to the back of the Gallery, I knew this would be a real test of our diction and audibility.

Also I reflected that we were bringing the Scottish play to Scotland…

There we didn't get entire acclaim.

DK in *The Bulletin* didn't like it much at all.

If the acting matched the production the new *Macbeth* would be really memorable… Film-star, Michael Redgrave has been too long in the studios… The more important small parts are competently filled.'

But the *Daily Express* (Robin Millar) thought differently:

'Magnificent *Macbeth*… This is a production so manly and vigorous, so lucidly spoken… Redgrave can rival any actor of the day in this part… Two scenes would bring tears from a stone, Macduff learning of his family's murder and the death of Malcolm's son – Clement McCallin and Leonard White deserving praise. It is Shakespeare on a scale you can rarely hope to see.'

A good review which I have copied word for word. But a shame in that unfortunately Malcolm is credited as having a son! I was not aware of that and especially not reporting his death. Nevertheless I am glad that I was 'deserving praise'.

In the *Glasgow Herald*, the review judged Michael Redgrave's performance to be 'uneven' but goes on, 'but this is a most sensitive reading of the part and many of its introspective passages are beautifully spoken… Ena Burrill dominated her scenes with a Lady Macbeth who pulsates with evil ambition… Leonard White made an unusually good Malcolm and his difficult scene with Macduff at the English Court was effective as it seldom is.'

The Scotsman had some reservations but, 'from the moment of the murder to his vigorous and brilliantly played duel with Macduff (Clement McCallin) [Redgrave's] performance gathered strength and force and terminated as a magnificently powerful piece of acting. Among the colleagues who maintained the Redgrave standard were Michael O'Halloran (Duncan), Leonard White (Malcolm) and Michael Goodliffe (Banquo).'

I have to write that I was especially pleased to get good "notices" in Scotland.

Birmingham's Theatre Royal came next, where for the first night according to MFK Fraser in the *Evening Despatch*, 'An ominous expanse of empty boxes and so much paper in the stalls, that the house rustled when it stood for The King… It will be a pity if Birmingham continues indifferent throughout the week, for Norris Houghton's production deserves to be seen, both in its own right and because of the impeccable acting with which it is sustained.

'Abundant talent in support of the talented principals, Michael Goodliffe (Banquo), Clement McCallin (Macduff), Leonard White, as Malcolm (his scene with Macduff in England done finely), are outstanding.'

The Weekly Post also gave me a lift and helped my confidence in these early days among such experienced and fine talents:

'The Malcolm of Leonard White was full of colour, and a much more vital personality than usually portrayed in the Scot's King's son.'

Lastly, on the road, the Theatre Royal in Newcastle-upon-Tyne, geared us for London. *The Northern Echo* reviewing: 'They give a magnificent interpretation.'

At this time the role of Duncan was changed to be played by Paul Stephenson. I cannot remember why this happened.

After a short break of ten days we opened at the Aldwych Theatre on December 18 1947, for a 'limited season'. and came under the scrutiny of the London press.

Alas, some were not so impressed.

WA Darlington in the *Daily Telegraph*, in spite of calling it 'An exciting *Macbeth*', went on to write, 'only once during the evening did the play rise above the plane of melodrama and soar into that of tragedy, and that was in a scene when neither of the two chief players were on the stage. It was the scene where Clement McCallin as Macduff, received the news of his wife's murder. 'Not many of the smaller parts in this play are very rewarding, but Michael Goodliffe's Banquo, deserves praise. And there must be a word for Leonard White's Malcolm…'

Then PLM in the *Daily Herald*:

'The first half was a marvel of correct lifelessness… Things woke up with the lusty heroics of Clement McCallin and Leonard White both fine as Macduff and Malcolm.'

But, Ivor Brown in *The Observer* congratulates Michael Redgrave: 'He brings to that terrifying part fine physique, a resonant voice, a sense of rhetoric, and an admirable willingness to take the knocks of really violent stage-fights.'

Elspeth Grant in the *Daily Graphic* only wrote about three of the players:

'Given two players so physically well equipped as Michael Redgrave and Ena Burrill to play the title role and Lady Macbeth, one, perhaps rashly, hoped for poetic performances of matching stature… They were not forthcoming… Mr Redgrave improved as he supped full of horrors and letting the neurotic supplant both soldier and poet, ended the play in triumphant defeat. Leonard White as Malcolm brought some freshness and light to a production otherwise unrelentingly sombre to the point of monotony.'

I became very self-conscious with that review. I was proud of course, but I wished that I'd not been picked out in contrast and in that way.

Things changed.

As soon as Norris Houghton had left us and returned to America Michael Redgrave started to call new rehearsals. He wanted to make changes in the England scene.

This being the scene that had been getting good reviews.

Clem McCallin wondered what this was all about?

I, so less experienced, just did as I was told.

Redgrave wanted to re-stage the scene. He wanted me to relax on a rostrum – at one point to be lying down, during the dialogue I am telling Macduff of the murder of his wife and children! I found this a fundamental change and quite impossible. It wouldn't work and I wanted to keep it in the way that had been successful. It was difficult for me to handle, but fortunately Clem McCallinn was adamant that it was not going to work. He stood up for me.

Nothing was resolved by the end of that rehearsal, and we went on playing the scene as originally staged by Norris Houghton, and Michael didn't call that rehearsal again.

But we didn't get to go to New York with the production.

Famous critic, JC Trewin (*John O'London's Weekly*, January 9, 1948), wrote: 'Leonard White speaks Malcolm's self accusation as cogently as I have ever heard it.'

My contract – it was for £20 per week – carried an option for a transfer to New York. That option was not taken up.

Indeed, the Lady Macbeth of Ena Burrill, was re-cast and Flora Robson took over for Broadway.

In fact only Redgrave and Hector MacGregor, who played Ross from the original cast, made the trip to the States.

Whatever; my first two years since de-mob and my serious experience of being a professional actor in Theatre, had proved quite happily worthwhile. More than I could really have hoped.

A season at Stratford-upon-Avon, working with top stars, top Directors and in fine plays, and with four important roles in the West-end. For me it all added up to a much better than normal start.

Would it last?

What next?

Chapter Five

Back to Basics?

Ignoring those six years I was in the Army, now by the end of 1947, I had been able to visit London theatre productions for some four or five years.

A great learning experience. Influences galore. A strong excuse to explore those heady times.

Looking through my programme records it appears that I saw about eighty shows during that period.

Out of that listing, my visits to the Old Vic were numerous. All impressive. Especially of course the young Laurence Olivier in Tyrone Guthrie productions. The entire version of *Hamlet*, and, with Alec Guinness and Jessica Tandy (what a lovely young actress) in *Twelfth Night*, Olivier again as *Henry V* – and in *Othello* with Ralph Richardson.

Also at the Old Vic, Guthrie directing Shaw's *Pygmalion* with Diana Wynyard, Robert Morley and Jay Laurier (what an excellent clown Jay Laurier was. He could bring the house down by just sweeping the stage!). And Guthrie continued in charge of *Measure for Measure* with Emlyn Williams and Marie Ney.

Also, *Richard III*, again with Emlyn Williams; Angela Baddeley was in that cast.

Michel Saint-Denis directing Olivier as *Macbeth* with Judith Anderson as the Lady. Esme Church directing Olivier and Alexander Knox in Bridie's *The King of Nowhere*. Bridie's "play for today", it seemed then.

Lewis Casson (Mr Sybil Thorndike) directing Olivier and Vivienne Bennett in *Coriolanus* (a partnership that went beyond on stage).

Later Guthrie directed another version of *Hamlet*, again "entire". But this time in modern dress, with Alec Guinness and Hermione Hannen.

And then Ibsen's *An Enemy of the People*, with Edward Chapman, Roger Livesey and Norah Nicholson, moving away from the Elizabethan.

Perhaps coincidental, during the war years the Old Vic moved its productions to the Golders Green Hippodrome, presenting Shaw's *The Devil's Disciple*, directed by Esme Church, with Stewart Granger, Sonia Dresdel, Andrew Cruickshank and Robert Donat.

Another GBS; *Saint Joan*, John Gielgud directed and also acted with Constance Cummings, Sonia Dresdel and Max Adrian.

John Gielgud also directed and was Earnest in *The Importance of Being...* with Jack Hawkins, Edith Evans, Gwen Ffrangcon Davies, Peggy Ashcroft, Margaret Rutherford (was it ever bettered?).

I then saw for the first time, the credit of Murray Macdonald directing the Old Vic Company at Golders Green, doing *Romeo and Juliet* with Robert Donat and Constance Cummings.

Later still the Old Vic company moved to the West End, to the New Theatre (later re-named the Albery), where I saw Ralph Richardson direct *King Richard II* with Alec Guinness and Harry Andrews.

Altogether, the Old Vic company was a strong influence on me over those inspiring years. I aspired to be with that Company one day... But I never was.

Many moons later I did do an audition on the true Old Vic stage for a part in *The Shoemaker's Holiday*, but I didn't get it. It wasn't 'my' play anyway. But I was disappointed.

I reasoned with myself that perhaps I didn't fit in rather than it being any assessment of my performance. Any excuse, I suppose.

My old programmes also reveal other influences, from other theatres and more modern works.

Black Limelight (Gordon Sherry) starring Margaret Rawlings, at the St James's – *Housemaster* (Ian Hay) with Joan White (no relation, but a good friend over many years) at the Shaftesbury.

Remarkably one line from that play has stuck in my mind for over fifty years, and it isn't remarkable at all now, it just made me laugh… A schoolboy joke. Something to do with knickers.

Shocking then! How things have changed…

Then, heavier fare, *Judgment Day* at the Phoenix Theatre, directed by Murray Macdonald with Freda Jackson and Glynis Johns.

That Elmer Rice play certainly impressed me, and started a long line of American plays that interested me greatly, and gave me a whole new experience of the modern theatre of that time.

You Can't Take It With You (Kaufman and Hart) at St James's with AP Kaye and Hilda Trevelyan, directed by William McFadden – *Mourning Becomes Electra* (Eugene O'Neill), with Laurie Cowie and Beatrix Lehmann, directed by Michael Macowan at the New Theatre.

Amphitryon '38 (Behrman/Giroudoux), starring Alfred Lunt and Lynne Fontaine, at the Lyric, directed by Bretaigne Windust.

Then, essentially American, was Clifford Odets' *Golden Boy* at the St James's, with Luther Adler, Lee J Cobb, Lilian Emerson and Morris Carnovsky, directed by Harold Clurman.

I saw this play twice at that same theatre. The second time with a change of director, Stella Adler, and different names in the cast, which included Louis Calhern, Eric Linden, Jo Schoengold and Jack La Rue. 'I wanna piece of that boy.'

Then the famous Steinbeck *Of Mice and Men* at the Apollo, with the excellent Niall MacGinnis, John Mills and Claire Luce, directed by Norman Marshall.

Clare Boothe's *The Women* at the Lyric, directed by Gilbert Miller, with Doreen Lang and Joan Greenwood.

Eugene O'Neill's *SS Glencairn*, which was at the small Mercury Theatre, directed by Robert Henderson, with Philip Dale, Anthony Booth. Anthony Sharp and Connie Smith in the cast.

The Mercury Theatre, in spite of its small size had a big reputation, playing an important part in launching *New plays by Poets* among its many successes.

That, of course, was when language and imagination created the unique role of theatre to inspire, to enhance, to suspend disbelief.

The American influence in my theatre-going during that time continued with Arthur Miller's *All My Sons*, seen at the Globe Theatre. It was directed by Warren Jenkins with Joseph Galleia and Margot Gilmore in the leads.

And, although theatre of a very different sort, a special highlight was my visit to the London Palladium to see Danny Kaye give us his one-man-show. A tour-de-force. He held the audience for a very long time spell-bound. For hours, yet never a dull moment.

What an act! What a lesson in stage-craft…

Apart from the highlights of the Old Vic productions and then the fresh and very different styles from America, there were of course other productions that cause me to linger in my rummage through the old theatre programmes…

Old Music by Keith Winter in which Greer Garson appeared with Hugh Williams and Celia Johnson. A rare work here for Margaret Webster who directed.

The popular *George and Margaret* (Gerald Savory), with Nigel Patrick, Irene Handl, Jane Baxter and Joyce Barbour at Wyndhams Theatre.

James Mason in Dodie Smith's *Bonnet Over The Windmill*, directed by Murray Macdonald. Mason became one of my top-ten actors.

Then three new plays by JB Priestley: *Time and the Conways* (one of his *Time* plays) at the Duchess Theatre, starring Jean Forbes Robertson and Mervyn Johns and directed by Irene Hentschel. *People at Sea* at the Apollo, directed by Auriol Lee, with Edward Chapman and Vivienne Bennett, and the remarkable *Johnson over Jordan*, with Ralph Richardson and Edna Best, directed by Basil Dean.

Contrasts by such writers as Karel Capek and Ernst Toller with *Power and Glory* (Oscar Homolka and Felix Aylmer), and *No More Peace* (a big multi-setting epic with large cast led by Vida Hope). All enhanced my early influences enormously.

I remember being very impressed by the performance of Jessica Tandy in Norman Macowan's (Michael Macowan's father) *Glorious Morning*, with Herbert Lomas at the Duchess Theatre. Claud Gurney directed that.

I also remember vividly, the young Stephen Haggard's performance in *The White Guard* (Bulgakov/Rodney Ackland) at the Phoenix Theatre. Also in that strong cast were,

Michael Redgrave, and Peggy Ashcroft. It was directed by Michel Saint-Denis.

Emlyn Williams writing, directing and playing the lead in *The Corn is Green* with Sybil Thorndike, at the Duchess.

Noël Coward changing course with his *Peace In Our Time*, which he co-directed with Alan Webb at the Lyric Theatre. In the cast were Kenneth More, Ralph Michael, Dora Bryan, Dandy Nichols and Alan Badel.

Kitty Black translating J-P Satre's *Crime Passionel*, which Peter Glenville directed at the Hammersmith Lyric. Joyce Redman was so good in that production, with Roger Livesey and Michael Gough.

Glenville also gave us *The Gioconda Smile* (Aldous Huxley) at the New Theatre, with Clive Brook, Pamela Brown, Marie Ney, Brenda Bruce.

Tony Hancock in Panto! *Cinderella* written by Frank Shelley, at the Dolphin Theatre in Brighton, Directed by Hal Burton.

Donald Wolfit, playing in (and co-directing with Christopher Ede) *The Merchant of Venice*, with Rosalind Iden at the Winter Garden Theatre.

A galaxy of names to conjure with. All challenging.

Hattie Jacques and Stuart Burge in *The King Stag* (Carlo Gozzi) at the Lyric Hammersmith.

Auden and Isherwood's *The Ascent of F6* – directed by Kay Gardner and Leonard Crainford at the Tavistock Rep (London).

Edna Best, Jack Hawkins and Bernard Miles in *Can We Tell?* (Robert Gore-Browne) at the New Theatre.

Ann Todd, Edmund Gwenn, Dorothy Hyson, Alan Webb – *She Too Was Young* at Wyndhams.

Leslie Banks, Constance Cummings – *Goodbye Mr Chips*, Shaftesbury Theatre.

Edith Evans, Owen Nares – *Robert's Wife* at the Globe.

Lucie Mannheim (she also directed), Marius Goring – *The Last Straw*, at the Comedy.

Naunton Wayne, Basil Radford – *Clutterbuck* at Wyndhams.

And there were many more, But what a rich vein of talent at that time to hopefully enhance my endeavours and set such high standards.

The challenge was truly stimulating…

But enough for now of this rummaging through my old programmes.

After my Malcolm in Michael Redgrave's *Macbeth* at the Aldwych, what then?

It was the beginning of my totally unplanned work in the new media.

Television at Ally Pally (Alexandra Palace), the BBC's early studios with the ominous transmitting aerial stuck on top of that building, like a "conning-tower", overlooking Alexandra Park racecourse.

Beaming to the rest of the world. Live of course. Magical, then. A miracle one might say.

Drama continuity there and then as for a theatre performance, and no recording as for a repeat, unlike cinema.

Later some form of primitive "tele-recording" (kinescope) was done by just placing a 16mm film camera in front of a TV monitor, but that was used only as a reference if at all necessary.

Live, being essentially the magic of being able to see beyond natural vision – god-like. Seeing is believing? A unique human experience. And therein lies the problem? Make-believe, perhaps?

That whole experience in the studio was, to say the least, cumbersome. Heavy lighting, heavy cameras, special make-up and unbearably hot often.

The first production for me to experience was in John Masefield's verse drama *Good Friday*, and no surprise it was broadcast on Good Friday (March 26, 1948). Produced by Douglas Allen. The cast included, Clement McCallin, playing Pontius Pilate, Margaretta Scott – Procula, and with, among a big cast, John Byron, John Boxer, Derek Hart, Oliver Burt and Michael Kent.

I played Longinus the Roman Centurion, and had that marvellous speech to Pilate relating the crucifixion…

'We nailed him there, aloft between the thieves in the bright air…'

The setting was by James Bould, and the Crowd was directed by Charlotte Bidmead.

That baptism was an exhilarating experience. To be part of the magic. Historic in fact.

However, getting back to the basics of Repertory, I then, in May 1948, had the chance to join the company at the Intimate Theatre, Palmers Green, in North London (just down the hill from Ally Pally) under the management of Frederick Marlow and producer (director) James Grant Anderson.

It was good additional training, no nonsense.

Although weekly turn-around with the plays, the company was large enough to be able to avoid everyone being cast on a weekly basis. For the first three plays in which I was appearing I was able to do them in a week-on, week-off pattern.

But nevertheless still with only one week in which to rehearse each play.

The first (May 7, 1948) was *Painted Sparrows* (Guy Paxton/Edward V Hoile), in which I played a character called Tom Lambert. Popular fare.

In the cast were, Ernest Haines, Kenneth Cleveland (who later became a successful Agent), Diana Fairfax, Toke Townley, Betty Bowden, Margaret Peplar, Robert Long and Enid Hewett.

Then two weeks later it was Warren Chetham-Strode's *The Day is Gone*, and in that cast were, David Raven, Barbara Hemingway, Robert Sansom, Monica Stutfield, Marjorie Zeidler and Sheila Storri.

Toke Townley, with me, were the only two from the first play I had been in at the Intimate.

The audiences could maintain a rapport with the players but not necessarily on a weekly basis.

Inspector Ernest Webb, was one of my early Police roles in which I found myself being cast. Hardly attractive. Usually one of the most unrewarding characters to play, because they often are the most difficult in which to learn the lines. They constantly lead the dialogue (question, question) having, more often than not, no "feed" on which to rely for response. The character *Frost* of that ilk was a richer much later invention, and not for Theatre.

Thankfully, the *Palmers Green-Southgate Gazette* reviewer VVD thought my role was 'extremely well conveyed'.

So that was some consolation.

But it was all ephemeral.

Soon on to the next, and that carried an unexpected bonus.

It was James Parish's *Distinguished Gathering*, in which I played CD Williams. During its normal run in the theatre, one of our performances provided an Outside Broadcast for BBC television...

A visit to the Intimate Theatre, Palmers Green on July 8th, 1948.

At 7.15pm, that evening, our audience in the theatre, was augmented by the larger audience in their homes watching the live transmission from just up the hill at Ally Pally. A new experience for us on stage, having cameras in the theatre, and all the paraphernalia of the Outside Broadcast crew around.

No chance in those days and under those conditions to make any of the adjustments for being on camera. What the TV audience got was the actor playing to the back row of the gallery, and that in the unreal theatre setting.

Suspension of disbelief was inappropriate for the TV viewer under those circumstances.

One of the pioneers of BBC TV drama, Campbell Logan looked after it for the transmission. The rest of the cast included, David Raven, Betty Cooper, Michael Gover, Betty England, Barbara Hemingway, Enid Hewitt, Ernest Haines, Vivienne Burgess, Roger Delgado, Toke Townley, and Roy Purcell.

Looking through my old programme, I see...

'NOTE: Members of the audience are kindly requested not to divulge the plot of *Distinguished Gathering* to any of their friends since this will obviously detract from the enjoyment of those who have yet to see the play.'

The TV transmission of the play on that day will have, unfortunately, blown that request!

Next, back to normal on August 2nd, was Barré Lyndon's, *The Man In Half Moon Street* in which I played Superintendent Warren. Another of those unrewarding roles – especially in weekly Rep as I have described.

In that cast were a few new names to the Company, Jack May, Peter Ducrow and Walter Plinge.

"Walter Plinge", of course, didn't exist. It was only a pseudonym used when the actor filling in playing a bit part didn't want to be acknowledged.

Miracle of miracles, Walter Plinge could have been playing in several different plays and different theatres in different towns throughout the country at the same time.

I wonder, if when it was a female character and therefore an actress being named in this way, an actress in the same situation, what she might be called? I never came across her.

"Vera Plinge" perhaps? Wife of the well-known actor, Walter?

A week later, it was *A Comedy of Woman*, John Van Druton's *The Distaff Side*. The women were, Dorothy Dewhurst, Enid Hewitt, Brenda Walter, Margaret Peplar, Elizabeth Gott, and Sheila Storri. Among the M players new to the company was Hugh Kelly.

I played Toby Chegwidden and my interpretation was described by the Reviewer in the local *Gazette* as 'an earnest suitor and an impressive temporary invalid'.

So, now you know (I don't!).

Next (August 16th, 1948) marked the seventh anniversary of the Theatre, and we played a revival of Frederick Marlow's *The Last of Mrs Cheyney*.

Noel Gordon made her first appearance at the Intimate playing Mrs Cheyney. I played the Hon. Willie Wynton ('Nuff said!).

That run made three plays in three weeks for me, and ended my season (May until August) at the Intimate Theatre in Palmers Green.

Not a time for deeply perfected performances, but a rich part of the learning curve, which now, alas, is rarely available to young trainees, some sixty years later.

Any revival of that system is perhaps too scary and too much trouble to contemplate by today's Producers and Players?

And the audience has probably gone anyway. But what a pity.

Almost immediately after that happy spell, enabling me to live at home in Finsbury Park, with Margaret and young son Martin, he now over four years old and starting school in Blackstock Road,

I then went from being in six different plays in the same theatre to do but one play in some twenty-three different theatres.

Touring.

Noël Coward was re-visiting an old work of his which hadn't been seen since 1925, when it was played by Tallulah Bankhead and Edna Best – his *Fallen Angels*.

He had given the opportunity to two young, first-time Producers, Lance Hamilton and Charles Russell, to try it out on the road.

We opened on October 4th 1948 at the Theatre Royal in Brighton, the theatre run so successfully at that time by J Baxter Somerville, with the excellent Jack Keates.

Before that, we had a problem. We had been rehearsing with the French actor Claude Serre in the role of Maurice Duclos, but he did not open with the play (and I don't know why).

David Peel, who was our director, stood in and played that role to begin with. However, not long after, by the second week in fact, Dennis Wood had taken over.

But *Fallen Angels'* success depends entirely on the ladies.

In this case Hamilton and Russell's new company was set up 'determined to demonstrate that talent is being overlooked.'

They cast Kathleen Kent, Diana Lincoln in the leads, with Gail Kendal playing the important Saunders the Irish maid.

They were excellent

John Wyndham and I played the husbands.

After Brighton we played, Cheltenham, Southport, Reading, Bath, Margate, Newcastle, Norwich, Harrow and Bournemouth.

Not necessarily in that order.

It went well enough for a second tour to be organised to follow.

Diana Allen took over then from Kathleen Kent.

We played Brighton twice. The second time at the Dolphin Theatre (next door to the Royal). Then, Blackpool, Torquay, Newport, Burnley, Leicester, Hull, Eastbourne, Huddersfield, Morecombe, Didsbury, Exeter and Glasgow.

It was interesting at this time in that I had joined an Agency known as Denis Wellesley, which of course was Viscount Dangan. And by the time I was getting my contract for the second tour of *Fallen Angels*, Terry Plunket Greene had joined them.

A happy time.

Between the two tours, I managed to do another television drama at Alexandra Palace studios. On Christmas Eve, 1948.

It was the Nativity play written by Dorothy L Sayers, called *He That Should Come*. Produced (directed) by Douglas Allen. Not a massive role (Second Shepherd) but I was glad that Douglas had called me again, and with a splendid cast comprising, Oliver Burt, Geoffrey Dunn, Glyn Lawson, Maurice Bannister, Christopher Gill, Willoughby Gray, Hugh Moxey, Stanley Lemin, Elizabeth Maude, Joseph O'Conor, Joanna Horder, Alan Wheatley, Andrew Leigh, Frank Coburn, John Vere, Evelyn Moore, Peter George, Kenneth Cleveland, Anna Somerset...

Also, I see a note in my scrapbook that at this time I was elected a Vice-President of Argosy, the amateur Drama Society of Uxbridge. A group that I'd enjoyed seeing on occasions when I'd been adjudicating drama festivals and also conducting some training sessions for Middlesex County Council activities at their Battle of Britain House, in Northwood.

Argosy were a very strong and talented group. I was proud to be associated with them.

1949 marked another special year for us on the home-front.

Between the two tours of *Fallen Angels* our second son,

Stephen Grant White was born on June 8th. Margaret nearly produced him at the Coliseum Theatre the day before when we had gone to see Doris Day in a matinee of *Annie Get Your Gun*. The excitement produced certain signs of an early birth! Next day, prematurely he arrived in the City Hospital, near the Angel, which, if the wind is in the right direction, and one has a strong enough imagination, is 'within the sound of Bow Bells'. And so a Cockney.

I was not present at the birth. That practise had not become the "done thing" then. I was back in the flat at Finsbury Park, looking after five-year-old Martin.

I remember sitting up in bed that morning and calling across to him on the other side of the room, (we only had one bedroom), 'You've got a brother'.

I believe that he only turned over in his bed…

He was probably thinking more about getting to school in Blackstock Road. And why wasn't Mother there to help?

So, then we were four. Three M and only one F in our cast-list.

I often wonder if Margaret, on an occasion such as that, didn't wish that I'd kept my word and not gone into acting.

I'd certainly been lucky so far, in getting much of my work close to home, but at this time I was heavily into touring, and then coming up, a spell of living in digs in Coventry.

With a lively five-year-old lad – Martin – and the new baby Stephen, Margaret coping on her own in those inappropriate top-floor rooms in Wilberforce Road N4 could not have been her ideal idea of married life.

Fortunately those occasional possible visits to her relatives (Aunty Wyn and Uncle Ern) in beautiful Somerset (Wellington) were very very welcome escapes for her and the boys.

But to Coventry, and all that, for me…

Things had progressed under the early days of the Arts Council, with Drama Director, John Moody, to move from weekly Rep and create a number of Civic Playhouses and companies allowing three-weekly turn-around in production.

Higher standards and a wider range of plays.

One such was the Midland Theatre Company based in Coventry.

Not only did it play in the "home" College Theatre, but it also toured to Nuneaton, Netherton and Redditch, while preparing the next production.

I had the good fortune to join that Company in September '49.

The Producer-Director, was Anthony John, and Basil Coleman was his Assistant Producer who joined at the same time as I did. It was a fine Company to work with:

Joy Harvey, Sheila Sweet, Graham Stark, Patricia Croft, Edward Dentith, Keith Lee, Edward Waddy, Christine Bennett, Benedicta Leigh, Gerard Burke, Griffith James, Howard Malpas, Peter Banks, David Buxton, Alan Toff, Rosamond Burne, Jane Comfort, Desmond Tester, Norma and Sheila Rudge, Judith Craig, Barbara Graley, Donald Cashfield, David Marlowe, Ronald McMaster, Patricia Brent, Robert James, Michael Barrington, Vera Harley, Geoffrey Edwards, P H Alexander and Edward Jewesbury.

A large group, not all used throughout the season, but it does illustrate that it was then possible to put on a production needing a large cast, and not to be avoided as so often nowadays.

The opening play of that, the fourth season, was Roland and Michael Pertwee's *The Paragon* on September 12th for its first week in Coventry, and then touring Nuneaton for three nights, Netherton three nights and Redditch for six nights.

It had quite a civic show-off celebration on its first night at which the local newspapers reported. Civic representatives and guests from Birmingham and London were present… Among Anthony John's guests were Mr Llewellyn Rees (Administrator of the Old Vic Theatre Company), Mr Michael Langham, Producer at Birmingham Repertory Theatre, the Mayor and Mayoress of Coventry, Mr John Moody, (drama Director of the Arts Council), Mr Tom Harrison (Midlands Regional Director, Arts Council), Mr HJ Dunkerley (BBC Midlands Regional Director), and Miss Nancy Burman (Productions Manager to Shakespeare Memorial Theatre)

In *The Paragon*, I played the leading role of the Unknown Man… and it all went well. The *Birmingham Post* reviewer reported that …

'A newcomer, Leonard White, displayed fine and sensitive acting in the exacting role of Simon…' So, I guess I'd made my mark in this new environment?

Next we played *Musical Chairs* (Ronald Mackenzie):

'Perfidious goings on in an oil prospector's bungalow isolated among the Galacian peaks…'

Basil Coleman took over as Director (Producer in those days) for this play, and the cast introduced Benedicta Leigh (October 3rd).

Basil had a fine CV to bring to this company.

Re-reading the programme notes of that play I am surprised to discover that he was born the same year as me – in the mid-first world-war years. Director Norman Marshall spotted him and gave him the lead in *Private History* at the Gate Theatre in London – then two seasons at the Old Vic – Tyrone Guthrie made him Assistant Producer for Benjamin Britten's version of *The Beggar's Opera* – Basil then produced Britten's *Rape of Lucretia* and *Let's Make an Opera*.

Many moons later our paths crossed again, in Toronto and then in Television at ABC (Teddington). More of that anon.

But there in Coventry so much earlier I was directed by him in playing a very difficult role – Joseph Schindler in *Musical Chairs*.

'The chief psychological study is a taciturn embittered ex-airman who believes his bombs killed his German fiancée.' That's how the character was described.

The *Coventry Standard* recorded that my impersonation was 'perhaps more of the spoiled child than the justifiable neurotic'.

The *Coventry Evening Telegraph* (JRC) thought that I fitted 'somewhat awkwardly into [my] second unsympathetic role… But he puts a great deal of intensity into the part.'

But Nuneaton liked my efforts better: 'From gentle Bach-playing moments at the piano, he explodes into vile displays of temper and cynicism – and he is not above stealing the affections of his brother's American fiancée and making her his mistress, Leonard White drew this character with rare sympathy and understanding…'

I don't play the piano, so I'm glad I got away with it!

But we didn't get away with it for all.

DC Whimster, JR Bennett, YH Price and Dr Hill – (Headmaster and three of the Staff) – writing to the Press from King Edward VI School, protested.

They wrote to the Press (*Observer*): 'This seemed to us a thoroughly bad play, both artistically and morally, in which vice is shown as noble and virtue as tiresome, ludicrous and dull… The youth of Nuneaton have been encouraged to develop the play-going habit, in preference to the cinema, and then are shown a play which is morally below the level of most films.'

And Arnold F Dauncey of the Headless Cross Rectory (what an address!) wrote to the *Redditch Indicator* twice. He begins by quoting from Princess Elizabeth 'We live in an age of falling moral standards…' and develops: 'The play "Musical Chairs" can only hasten this decline in morality. It is deplorable that State aid should be used to finance such plays which portray immorality and loose sexual relationship as something of no consequence. The pity is that such excellent talent should be wasted on the presentation of such low-standard plays.'

But he did go on to write that 'Both the production and the acting were first class.'

After the run in Coventry, BBC Radio broadcast excerpts from the production on October 10th 1949. It was introduced by TC Kemp of the *Birmingham Post* and produced for the BBC by William Hughes. It was broadcast at 7.15pm in "family listening time", and so I can only think that the excerpts or discussion of the play must have cut out all the immorality. Although I doubt very much that the broadcast would have mis-represented the type of play it was. That being so, for the tour at least, there must have been sufficient warning to 'protect the young'.

Although I have no memory of it being done, I gather from a press-cutting that, in Redditch on the first night, the Manager, at the end of the performance 'advised parents not to bring their children to the production!'

After all that, the programme for the season didn't alter at all, but I guess it was fortunate that we were next into a double-bill by Terence Rattigan. More acceptable?

Entitled *Playbill*, it started with *The Browning Version*.

Set as it was in a Public School, possibly this may have been more like the stuff of serious drama for those who wrote about "Musical Chairs" from both the King Edward VI School and Headless Cross Rectory?

Certainly, a distinct contrast.

With, *Harlequinade*, Rattigan's unlikely burlesque of a 'Midlands Theatre company rehearsing *Romeo and Juliet*, described as a 'highly diverting frolic', it provided an 'Appetising Mixed Grill' (*Coventry Telegraph*). The full Company including the staff let rip in this 'romp'.

Certainly nothing there to complain about.

I played Frank Hunter in *The Browning Version* and Fred Ingram in *Harlequinade*. A nice double.

Next (November 15 1949), into the classics, and the Russian no less. Ivan Turgenev's *A Month in the Country*, a version by Emlyn Williams.

Basil Coleman continued his Direction in a work which the 'seasonal repertoire serves admirably to demonstrate the protean accomplishment of the Arts Council Midland Theatre Company', (*Birmingham Mail* November 21) falling is it did between Ronald Mackenzie's *Musical Chairs* and Basil Thomas's *Shooting Stars*, which was to follow.

The Turgenev play introduced a new young actor in fifteen-year-old, Alan Toff as Kolia. The *Coventry Standard* reported that his 'uninhibited enthusiasms, as the child of the house, relieved the morbid atmosphere'.

I wonder what happened to Alan Toff?

The *Midland Daily Tribune* reporter wrote: 'Serious-minded devotees of drama who saw the play, must recognise this classic as the most ambitious and worthwhile production of the current season. Never before have the players risen to such great dramatic heights. Never before have they acted with such inspired purity and expressive feeling as they do in this memorable production.'

Well, well! Full marks for Basil Coleman's influence.

Graham Stark, in his early "straight" days, played Beliaev.

I found the pensive character of Rakitin difficult. My performance seemed mostly to attract the description 'sensitive', 'sensitively portrayed', 'sensitively taken', by the Reviewers. I hope that was better than 'interesting'?

In the *Birmingham Mail* CLW went a bit further…

'Leonard White spoke and carried himself well as Rakitin'.

Then, contrasting, two comedies followed to take us up to the Christmas season.

First, *Shooting Star* by Basil Thomas, described as 'Fun at expense of Football – mirroring some of the back-room scenes of soccer – simply poking fun at the method of transfer deals…'

A bit before its time? Nowadays more likely perhaps to be the subject of tragedy in drama rather than comedy?

Set in 'a Midlands town, Burnville', it was brave of us to have a go at the local accent, and satisfy our particular audiences. The purists didn't think so, but undaunted we strove and just about got away with it.

Desmond Tester was introduced into the Company for this production.

In my part (a character role needing the balding hair-piece – not happily my style, but necessarily just part of the scope of the Rep actor of those days), I was described as bringing 'a little Black Country humour', which I hope contributed to the happy review:

'As a comedy the play really "scored" a bullseye – to send the audience home in thoroughly good humour.' (*Coventry Evening Telegraph*)

The Christmas production, continuing the happier theme, was an unlikely play, written as it was by the famous Theatre critic, WA Darlington. Following his *Alf's Button*, this one he called *Magic Slippers*.

In the bad joke department (I had some reputation for making bad jokes, probably demonstrated herein…) much later, at the Bristol studios of HTV, Christine Penwarden (make-up) told me that she was making a book of my bad jokes! Obviously a non-seller…

However, in that department, moving from *Shooting Star* to *Magic Slippers* was soccer-boots to carpet slippers in the wardrobe…

'A laugh in every line'. Hardly!

But to resume, Anthony John directed this 'admirable Christmas concoction' which again presented a large cast of twenty-one.

Not the conventional panto, but an outrageous story of the riotous consequences involving the wearers of a pair of carpet slippers that had been fashioned out of a supposed magic carpet.

Those slippers provided transport from the home of a Church-warden in Cookham to the harem of a Sheikh in the exotic East, and thus enabled the setting 'which rivalled a panto for spectacle'.

Add the dances arranged by Graham Stark (for himself, Vera Harley, Norma and Sheila Rudge), and the frolic, it resulted in 'a mad, merry and mirthful mixture'.

Certainly it fitted the seasonal bill: 'the play evoked uncontrollable outbursts of mirth which literally shook the hall' (*Midland Daily Tribune*).

I played the pompous villain in this, and I found how truly satisfying it was to play in a successful comedy, and to learn the important lesson that comedy has to be played seriously.

The audiences have to find the funny side, not the players.

Until I read my old notes again, I hadn't realised that originally a different play had been scheduled for this Christmas season.

The original intention apparently was to present *The Prisoner of Zenda*. However, it was reported that any 'disappointment was completely mitigated on acquaintance with *Magic Slippers* the subsequent choice... this fantastic comedy is a welcome successor.'

During this run the forties came to a close. I'd missed being at home for both the Christmas and the New Year. Not good.

With Martin now nearly six and Stephen six months, I ought to have been playing Father Christmas and helping Margaret put jest in the Fest. But no.

The wrong career?

I stayed at Coventry for the next two productions. 1950 started with RC Sherriff's *Miss Mabel*. Basil Coleman was back directing. Geoffrey Edwards and PH Alexander had joined the Company.

Back to the straight play involving 'a forged will, a touch of false impersonations and a murder'. Hardly original ingredients, but RC Sherriff wrote well.

I had the role of a young Doctor in this, a 'sincere doctor' and I have a most unpleasant memory of one performance when just at a critical moment – I had to deliver an important line and that was supposed to bring the curtain down. A cliff-hanger. Only, it didn't.

I was about to utter it when I caught my breath, and struggle as I might I just could not say a word...

A long, awful, pause. Only Geoffrey Edwards was on stage with me, and he couldn't help. I continued to splutter and regain my breath. But I just could not.

After what seemed like an age, eventually the curtain did come down, but, alas, without that important line of dialogue!

What the audience made of it I do not know. For me it was horrible.

Otherwise for the rest of the run, the reviews held up well.

'Performed for our delight by the Midland Theatre Company at the peak of their form' (*Nuneaton Observer*).

Well, I've probably only kept the good ones anyway.

The last show for me with that Company was unexpectedly special.

It was Hugh Walpole's *The Cathedral* (February 6, 1950), first written as a novel in 1922, and eventually adapted to a stage play.

Strong stuff, this Walpole tragedy of, 'a man whose blind and unbending pride leads him into a succession of sickening upheavals'.

Edward Jewesbury had joined the Company and was playing the leading role of Archdeacon Adam Brandon, whose damnation is the essence of the story following the arrival of Canon Ronder, with his modernistic views of Christianity.

I played 'Canon Ronder'. I welcomed this strong role to end my season with the Arts Council Midland Theatre Company.

The *Coventry Evening Telegraph* (JRC, February 7, 1950), recorded 'First rate acting in *The Cathedral*... As the modern churchman and perpetual thorn in Brandon's flesh, Leonard White skilfully plays the forthright and amiable Canon Ronder'.

DSH in the *Coventry Standard* thought it was 'one of my best roles'...

The local Nuneaton press reckoned that the production 'will rank as the Company's best dramatic performance to date... and fortunate for having Leonard White in the part of Canon Ronder'.

But, perhaps best of all, my scrap-book reveals, a lovely letter from a group of "permanent ticket-holders" from Netherton, Dudley, Worcestershire, who had seen every performance of mine...

'In every part you have given us acting of the very highest quality. Some of us saw you at Stratford in 1946, and we also remember an excellent performance as Malcolm in Michael Redgrave's *Macbeth*... we are extremely sorry that you are now leaving... We should be very pleased to welcome you back as guest actor at any time... May we offer you our very best wishes for your future success and grateful thanks for the pleasure you have given us.'

That was signed by a group of sixteen who had taken the trouble to write. So much appreciated.

Truly wonderful to have that assessment from the most important of all – the audience.

And from within the Company I received a beautifully designed hand-made card which opened to reveal a dozen separate sections each bearing signatures of 'Thank-you, love and good wishes'.

And so back happily to home. And also back to "resting", the inevitable in the 'biz...

***

The new decade started slowly. A revival (or rather a second performance) of John Masefield's *Good Friday* took me back to TV, for the Easter transmission. Unlike now when it would be the original recording just taken off the shelf and 'run VT', in those early days, the production had to be made all over again.

Better for the cast etc., because it meant another full fee – and maybe even a little more, instead of just a smallish residual, for the repeat. Sometimes not even that.

As it happened almost all the lead cast were the same as in the original, with Clement McCallin and Margareta Scott playing Pilate and Procula. One famous new name here was Lydia Sokolova who directed the crowd.

Douglas Allen was the Producer (Director) as before, and I was very happy to be invited back to play my original role, Longinus, the Centurion, and again deliver those wonderful Masefield lines relating the crucifixion to Pontius Pilate...

'God! It is a slow way to make die, a man, a strong man who can beget men…'

And then, back to basics, a touch of the non-pro theatre world. I was asked to Adjudicate in the National Festival of Community Drama, arranged by the British Drama League.

The Festival included companies from across the UK.

Gloucestershire, Llandrindod Wells, Ammanford, North Wales and Yorkshire. I adjudicated at the Gloucester and Scarborough centres.

Always stimulating, and interesting to see a wide variety of plays in a short space of time, and to test one's judgment.

Another view for the actor, to see others as others see us.

And the overall creativity.

Of all the departments to be assessed, I was always fascinated by the Choice of Play category. Often straightforward if it contained a juicy big role just right for Mr or Mrs So-and-So in a tried and tested piece, but more challenging if it's a new play written by the local budding Noël Coward or Alan Ayckbourn.

Unfortunately it so often was not.

As someone who much later was in a position to commission a great deal of new writing (ABC TV, *Armchair Theatre*), I hoped that I might see a new drama succeed. I tended to give a few extra marks for those brave enough to try the untried.

On this occasion in the Gloucestershire entries there was indeed a new play presented by Hucclecote Women's Institute, but in spite of my wishes for the new creation to succeed, it was Priestley who won. A tough competitor.

I was one of the early members of the then, newly formed, Guild of Drama Adjudicators, and over many years, when my pro work would allow I did enjoy getting back to my basics.

To stimulate, as best I could, all the good work of the Amateur Theatre.

Another branch of my basics was the Reunion Theatre Guild Ltd (Patrons Sir Laurence Olivier and Sir Bronson Albery) which on this occasion, put together a try-out of a new play by Hal D Stewart called *The First Victoria*.

Set in the days of the Iceni, AD 61, and Boadicea's trouble with the Romans, its reunion was not ours. We were only a get together following our more recent battles.

It was a history written for the 1950s in an unusual way, presenting the ancient past in modern dialogue and reflected situation.

The Producer was Bruno Barnabe, and the Décor by Gower Parks.

This cast included, Richard Johnson, Roderick Lovell, Walter Horsfall, Richard Caldicot, Oliver Burt, Pamela Alan, Milton Rosmer, Jan Pilbeam, and Elspeth March in the lead as Boodikka (the new phonetics!) – reviewed as 'a highly intelligent performance' – 'a first class performance'.

Elspeth's successful interpretation was perhaps a mixture of a Bessie Braddock of the modern past and a Margaret Thatcher more recently?

I played Sextus Lapidus ('Nuff said!).

Before opening at the Embassy Theatre in London, we had a short tour taking in the Festival Theatre at Malvern and The Arts Theatre, Cambridge.

I have only one strong memory of the first night. I had to open the play (top "in order of appearance") and my opening lines called for a reference to a certain prop on the set.

On that particular occasion I burst on, to impress, but, alas, alas, the important prop was not there... It had not been set.

Collapse of Sextus Lapidus! (And the opening of the play...)

Ah, the trials of live Theatre, but probably good training for live TV. No re-takes.

As it happened, live TV was again next. More Romans, and as it happened, more John Masefield, and more 'Produced by Douglas Allen'.

Was I getting typecast? Whatever, I happily seemed to be getting into Douglas Allen's TV Rep company. No complaints.

The play was *The Tragedy of Pompey the Great* and I was playing Cato.

I didn't know anything about that Roman gent, and must have confessed so to Margaret at home. As a result she wasn't going to have me look stupid at rehearsals and so she went to work on her research and came up with a fulsome biog of:

'Cato, Marcus... Roman Statesman (95-46 BC). Great-grandson of the Censor, Uticencis... served with distinction in the Spartacist insurrection... when the civil war broke out, he joined the party of Pompey... in continual opposition to Caesar... etc etc.'

Usually of course one expects to know enough about the character being played from the script itself, but in this case I guess I was pleased to be able to show-off a bit in rehearsal.

I'd done my homework. Well, Margaret had done it for me.

This was another good cast to be with. Among them, Isabel Dean, John Witty, Rachel Gurney, Jack Livesey, James Carney (who starred – top of the bill), George Skillan, Richard Caldicot, Robert Brown and Stanley Baker (who later was with me in probably the highlight of my acting career – more about that later).

We transmitted on Sunday, September 24, 1950, with a second performance the following Thursday.

Still on camera, next was a film called *The Dark Man*, produced by Julian Wintle. Julian continuing his very much appreciated support in my work. It was a Jeffrey Dell screenplay and he also directed it. A murder story and I played Detective Evans.

Certainly a change from the Roman toga.

The lead was played by Edward Underdown.

Not a very well-known but a good actor (I also knew him as an excellent gentleman jockey, "over the sticks". I followed him at a Plumpton race meeting once, but I don't remember winning anything).

In *The Dark Man* he was reviewed as 'excellent as the Detective Inspector (*Picturegoer Weekly*).

More well-known names in the cast were, Natasha Parry, Maxwell Reed, Barbara Murray, William Hartnell, Sam Kydd, Betty Cooper. Eric Cross was the Director of Photography.

The end of 1950 took me back to Theatre with a run in London, but starting with a try-out at the Theatre Royal in Brighton, my old local. Happily, I could play there from my old homestead in Newhaven, and better still, later, be with Margaret and the two boys (Martin now 6 and Stephen 20 months old) when we got to Town for the run.

London was always referred to as the Town.

The play was *Point of Departure* (the Jean Anouilh – *Orpheus & Eurydice*, translated by Kitty Black), starring Mai Zetterling, Dirk Bogarde and Stephen Murray.

We opened in Brighton on October 23rd 1950. I played the role of Mathias but also understudied Dirk's lead – Orpheus.

We transferred to the Lyric Theatre in Hammersmith in November, and then into the West End at the Duke of York's Theatre at the end of the year. So, thankfully Christmas at home that year and in work.

Good work too! Eighteen pounds per week (eight performances)

As I write now, the 21st Century intervenes and takes over. I've just taken a phone call from a friend. The voice said:

'I expect you've seen it?'

'What?'

'The obit... Christopher's obit, in the paper.'

Stunned.

'No, I haven't seen it. I didn't know that he had died!'

It was a couple of days before. Only a few days before that, Christopher had been on the phone to me, talking about our next get together... And now he was gone.

Christopher Fry had provided in the year of 1951 the turning point of my career, and as I come up to the description of that experience over half a century ago, I hear that he has gone...

He was a ripe old age, but he still was very active, young at heart... A wonderful dramatist. A wonderful man.

So now I pick-up in a different mood. The living link is severed. So very, very sad. But my words are inadequate...

My very good fortune was to be cast in Christopher Fry's play *A Sleep of Prisoners*, which he had written specially for the Festival of Britain. That wonderful celebration following the War.

Whatever, it was also a wonderful opportunity for me.

A Happy New Year ahead.

And what a challenging surprise to come.

1951 – Festival of Britain year.

Chapter Six

The Peak?

1951 – Festival of Britain year.

For me it started with the continuation of *Point of Departure* at the Duke of York's Theatre in London's West-end, playing Mathias and under-studying Dirk Bogarde's Orpheus.

It was all going well, until after a few weeks – February 8th to be precise – the totally unexpected happened.

At that performance, it was the end of Act 2, and as was the practise with any member of the cast not involved in Act 3, I was soon out of my costume. I had reported to the Stage Manager that, with the others in the same state, I was going across the road to the ABC tea-rooms for a cuppa. Ok, no problem.

Something like ten minutes later, while having the welcome cuppa and a natter with the others, waiting for Act 3 to have gone up, before going home… the SM came dashing into the teashop, calling to me as he ran…

'You're on!'

'What?'

'You're on! Dirk's sick – can't go on… QUICK!'

Quick indeed, without a thought, I'm running back to the theatre up to my dressing room and into my other costume – the one for Orpheus, down the stairs two at a time, on to backstage, a deep breath (or two) and I made my entrance as Orpheus… for Act 3!

The Act break had gone on much longer than usual and the audience were mystified, to say the least.

What they made of it, seeing the male lead role being played by two different actors in the same performance, was beyond me, especially as in my role of Mathias, I'd been killed off in the first Act. Anyway, I just got on with it and committed suicide for the second time, but this time as Orpheus.

If I'd had time to think about it, I'd have been mostly concerned for Mai Zetterling having to cope with this extraordinary situation.

But she was marvellous.

And at curtain-down (according to the *Daily Mirror* next morning), the audience gave me 'a great reception'.

Dirk was off for six performances, and so I got the chance (what a chance!) to play Orpheus throughout that time. But I was so sorry for Dirk. He was splendid in the role.

He played it for real at every performance, and tore himself apart in the process reliving the heavy emotional experiences.

On that first occasion when he couldn't go on after Act 2 he had become physically sick in his dressing-room, and just couldn't play the rest. For such a fine actor, it was strange that he seemingly lacked the technique to enable him to play in continuity night after night in the theatre, without tearing himself apart.

Eventually, as is now history, Dirk was more at home in Cinema film-making.

I had to keep going, under the emergencies, (and what a great challenge that was) but of course I was not a star name, and it became necessary to give time to rehearse a star replacement. To keep the show on the road.

Then, as soon as possible, Peter Finch took over the role of Orpheus. He did not seem to me to be confident in anticipation. But he was the new bright boy in Town.

As for me, I then left the cast, having had a truly very special offer. An offer which with hindsight turned out to be a turning point in my career. Denis Quilley took over my role in *Point of Departure*.

Quite out of the blue, so far as I was concerned, I was asked to be in the new play that Christopher Fry had written specially for the Festival of Britain. It was called *A Sleep of Prisoners* and the play called for a cast of just four men. Four equally large and important characters.

A truly wonderful anticipation.

The story was (is) complex, dealing with four soldiers who have just been taken as prisoners of war, and are temporarily, overnight, housed in a disused church in a no-mans-land of a war-zone. Resonant, but not specific, of World War II. During that night as they fitfully sleep, they dream, have nightmares perhaps. Each man's dream is demonstrated, and each involving the other three in episodes of violence.

These episodes are in fact specific occurences of different forms of violence from the Old Testament. And each stemming from the different characters and characteristics of the four men.

As, perhaps, they see each other.

Each actor has therefore in effect to play four roles, four aspects of his character. Complex indeed.

To this day I have no idea of just how I came to be selected for that casting. (I did hear many moons later that the actress Jessie Evans had suggested to Christopher that I do it, but why I do not know.) But I was mightily pleased, although I did not know then just how big the challenge was.

To begin with the irony of it all was extraordinary. It was to be directed by, Michael MacOwan, who, (I hope, you will remember) had been my Officer in charge, when I was in the Army Bureau of Current Affairs Play Unit, during my last months in the Army, and – to the point – had, when on my demob, I'd applied to him for a job (or reference) he had suggested that I might try Stage Management, rather than acting!

Now, he was, offering me this difficult role in a new and prestigious play for the Festival of Britain, and written by such a fine poet-dramatist as Christopher Fry.

Coming to meet in these now changed circumstances, Michael was full of enthusiasm! That was heart-warming, to say the least. I was glad that I'd not taken up his earlier advice and given up acting.

And so was he it seemed.

We knew at the start of rehearsals, the opening date and venue 'on the road'. It was to be April 23rd 1951 at the University Church in Oxford. The London venue had not been agreed. A church on the South Bank near Waterloo was someone's choice. We all went to inspect, but saw immediately it was quite wrong. It was in a pristine condition, all newly white painted on the exterior, and in splendid condition obviously for the Festival of Britain. Certainly not in any way suggestive of a bombed church as needed. London had certainly been horribly bombed, and we started a search for the ideal place.

The West End was not the obvious area, but surprisingly Michael and Christopher, found just the building in St Thomas's Church, Regent Street. It was described as 'in Regent's Street' but actually it was tucked in behind the shops and backed on to Rupert Street. Indeed the vestry of the church was separated across the road in that narrow back street. Our back-stage dressing room was in fact "back vestry".

More to the point and what made it just about an ideal venue was that it had been bombed at the altar end, and remained unrepaired with a huge tarpaulin slung across the roof to cover the bomb-hole.

We rehearsed in the West End in another church hall off Shaftesbury Avenue. An appropriate mix of church and theatre.

Christopher was with us the whole period, and that was wonderful. With such a text his presence and guidance gave us the very necessary authority. But he never imposed.

Never interrupted. More often than not he'd let us find our own way, until perhaps we would get stuck and be compelled to cry for help!

On those occasions he would give us a clue, not a directive, and remarkably simplify the situation.

Illustrating clearly, that the characters were true, were real, and not poetic contrivances. And especially to avoid the trap of trying to make his words sound like Shakespeare, which often had become a cheap and quite incorrect description of his works.

We learned to keep it grounded, and so much more powerful for that. It was never allowed to get reverential.

Jokes enlightened the environment of rehearsal. And my reputation for bad jokes even helped (me at least), particularly when I suggested on one occasion, a Te Deum should not become tedium. Ugh!

We were a tight quartet, Denholm Elliott, Stanley Baker, Hugh (Hwfa) Pryse and me. An inspired social group too, with Hugh Goldie (Associate Producer and Stage Director), Peter Vaughan (Stage Manager, and my understudy), Adza Vincent (General Manager – later on a very successful Agent). George Fearon was our Press Representative.

After long sessions of exploration in rehearsal, we'd continue happily, and relax, around the table at a nearby pub.

A Sleep of Prisoners was presented by Pilgrim Players Ltd for the Religious Drama Society. A credit of considerable prestige for them. A Festival of Britain production in association with the Arts Council of Great Britain.

The premiere was as planned on April 23rd 1951 in St Mary the Virgin Church in Oxford (an appropriate date?), and we had a short tour taking in Blackpool, Lancaster and Bournemouth before opening in London on May 15th in St Thomas's Church, Regent Street.

It wasn't just the Church as Theatre as of early days, but the Church being the actual setting, the location of the action.

It certainly provoked striking reviews. Unlike Fry's earlier Church plays – *Thor With Angels* etc. – this was contemporary with strong resonances so few years after World War II.

We all carried in our separate ways the unique experience of those six long years of the country at war.

Again my later memory of the shock of hearing of Christopher's death overtakes. We had been continually in touch for over fifty years; and only a short time before that so sad news we had been trying to arrange another get together…

I was very keen to try to get a video made of *Sleep* and Christopher was keen too… Such a great shame.

But back to 1951. The pre-London short tour of *A Sleep of Prisoners* was a sharp practice in adapting to the different church environments, and particularly varying settings, and the often poor acoustics. But, thankfully, we became quite expert in dealing with those problems. We had to be.

The Premiere in Oxford attracted wide attention, happily very appreciative. We knew then that we were, as we had always believed, involved in a rare, fine worthwhile experience of English theatre.

We, the Quartet, all got plaudits, but one review sticks in my memory. It was from the University journal, *Isis*.

The student reviewer took it to pieces: '*A Sleep of Prisoners* challenges the secular theatre on the religious theatre's ground, mixes up its rituals and emotions, dabbles in both medieval simplicity and modern subtlety, and fails…'

That reviewer was named Brian Tesler.

Little did I know then that the same Brian Tesler would turn up, twelve years later, quite by chance, to be my boss (Programme Controller) at ABC TV where I was Producing drama!

A small world.

I've often wondered since then if Brian ever remembered reviewing me as an actor ('Nor can one blame the actors for anything…') when we had our meetings in 1960 about *Armchair Theatre*? He certainly never mentioned it, and I never wanted to remind him of what we actors thought of his review in 1951.

A Sleep of Prisoners had a limited run in London before going on another tour of the country, taking in, Birmingham, Brighton, Bristol, Norwich, Eastbourne, Leeds, Ipswich and Bury St Edmunds. That last venue proved to be our sternest test acoustically in that vast pillared space. We then returned to London for a second run in St Thomas's, Regent Street, opening on July 31st. That ran on until the end of September.

During the London runs I found opportunities to get the family to my old home town, Newhaven, to enjoy the seaside and I used to commute daily. But I had two nasty scares. First when the train that I was on taking me to Victoria Station in London, usually getting me there in good time, decided on that occasion to crawl along getting slower and slower and later and later! Me seething meanwhile. Long before having a mobile phone and so being horribly out of touch. I was still en-route when I should have been opening the play. The Stage Manager, Peter Vaughan was my understudy and he went on in my place.

I felt terrible, but I fancy Peter was only too glad of the opportunity. And what an excellent leading character actor Peter went on to become. I consider it a great bonus to be able to record him being my understudy. Reflected glory!

And he had another opportunity to play my role of David King later on. I acquired a boil on my bum (the setting of the play used a lot of dirty loose straw, and that being not the best bedding. I guess I'd picked up something…). It was painful, and not congenial to all the action I had to perform. So I had to take a performance out.

Those were the only two "downs" for me during the whole of the eventual long run.

Probably the highlight was the special midnight matinee that was arranged so that the pros playing in other West-end productions could get to see us. It was magic. Not only the atmosphere of the deep summer night, but also because among the crowd of fellow-actors, we were honoured by Laurence Olivier and Vivien Leigh, who brought Fredric March and his wife, Florence Eldridge, with them. After the performance they came "back-vestry" to congratulate us. Quite an occasion. Being congratulated by our top stars as well as by Hollywood stars. I'd always been full of admiration for Vivien Leigh (especially as we shared the same birthday – a fellow Scorpio) and Fredric March was my number one film actor.

During the run of *Sleep* in London I managed to do some radio work. I was very fortunate in that BBC Producer Mary Hope Allen liked my work and booked me many times. At this time it was Third Programme material.

I was Arcadipane in *Lazarus* (Pirandello, translated by C Scott Moncrieff) with the likes of Robert Speight, Catherine Salkeld, Lewis Stringer, Martin Starkie, Patrick Troughton, Vivienne Chatterton and Denis Arundell…

Also, Books 5 and 9 of *The Aeneid*. Strong stuff for the ex-Council school boy?

Fortunately I was not needed to provide my CV when Mary cast me.

I also managed to do some Adjudicating of the Gloucestershire Community Council Drama Festival. Making sure that I kept my feet on the ground.

The run of *A Sleep of Prisoners* had gathered a wonderful collection of reviews (not to mention some inspired memento drawings, and show photographs).

'Mr Fry holds them with stirring faith and in *A Sleep of Prisoners* he makes the holding of them a moving and a noble experience. This without question is his best play.' (Harold Hobson, *Sunday Times*.)

'A moving and memorable experience. It should not be missed by anyone interested in the theatre or the church…The acting of Leonard White, Denholm Elliott, Stanley Baker, and Hugh Pryse carries the play triumphantly.' (*Sunday Dispatch*.)

'Would Shaftesbury Avenue could do so well!' (*Sunday Graphic*.)

'Flashing lines that lift the heart and make one thankful that we can have such a poet in our theatre.' (*Observer*.)

'For all its unduly complex treatment [Fry's] story has a compelling strength and beauty. It is acted with a burning zeal…' (Cecil Wilson, *Continental Daily Mail*.)

'Excellent performances… *Sleep of Prisoners* needs an article to itself. I have space here only to point out that Mr Fry shows himself to be a master of theatrical technique outside the prison of the proscenium.' (*Tribune*.)

'It is not only the most impressive Festival offering, but also one of the finest new plays of the year, and it is acted with much vitality and sensibility…' (Geoffrey Tarran, *London Morning Advertiser*)

'Fry's new play provides a most moving experience, and I strongly recommend it… No one should miss this. Michael Macowan – the Producer – matches the play with a remarkable ingenuity and a perfect feeling for its values, and the actors are all quite admirable.' (*New Statesman*.)

'This is in brief, a noble piece of work which I should have been a fool to have missed. It is in a high degree, intellectually and spiritually and even theatrically exciting. But will the true poet who wrote it now consider returning to the playhouse, at least for a time? England hath need of such big Fry.' (Alan Dent).

And there were many more…

Thus with such success, and still with work to do (with such challenging material one is continually striving to get the quartet right) the news came that a transfer to New York, Manhattan, was calling…

A tribute though that was, I was not altogether attracted to begin with. Especially as I hated any thought of our strong quartet being possibly broken up. I made a condition that I would sign the contract to go only if the original cast was being kept together.

Time was short. Only a matter of a few weeks before a proposed opening in New York.

The first blow was when I heard that Denholm Elliott would not continue as he had an offer for another production – also in New York, where he already had considerable credit.

So, I did not want to go.

The Agent, Gordon Harbord was handling the package representing the American producers (Luther Greene and the Francitas Film Foundation Inc.). He certainly put pressure on me to change my mind. It wasn't easy for me as I'd got so involved with the quartet as it was. And especially insofar as it was Denholm who was leaving. His role was extremely important in relation to mine.

Time was pressing.

I was told that the replacement for Denholm had been chosen. I had not heard of the actor before. He was a young Canadian, Donald Harron, who was playing at the Arts Theatre in London, and had impressed.

I was uneasy, but persuaded eventually to change my mind.

So Broadway here I come! Well not exactly, Broadway.

The Church that had been chosen was on Madison Avenue at 71st – 'St James'. It was my first crossing of the Atlantic and by air.

And that was some experience beyond the expected!

Margaret and the two boys accompanied me to Heathrow to wish me *bon voyage*. We didn't know how long I'd be away. So it was with very mixed feelings that I boarded the PanAm Stratocruiser…

That unique airliner of that time, a double-decker, with a lower deck that consisted of the bar-lounge. Rather more like an airship pod where you walked downstairs from the seating deck and went to the bar to order your drink and then sat around in seats looking out of the wide windows at the skyscape.

It was evening as we took off. Scheduled as then to stop at Shannon, where we would disembark for a full dinner in the restaurant at the airport. Thence across the pond to touch down again at Gander in Newfoundland. Disembark for a shave and morning cuppa, and then on to Idlewild, NY.

Well that was the schedule, but it didn't quite work out like that. In fact, not like that at all.

It was a lovely night as we climbed into a clear moonlit sky. Not long and we were over the Irish sea. I had a window-seat and was fascinated to look out at the moon, now not up above me but on my eyeline. I was truly in the heavens.

That is, I was, until I looked along the wing, on the starboard side, and noticed that one of the two propellers wasn't going around.

Strange! But nothing seemed amiss in the cabin. All relaxed. So I thought that this was normal and that after getting to cruising height, the Captain could 'rest' one of his engines? He had three others.

Stanley Baker was the only other member of the cast on that plane, and he was seated some rows behind me. I turned to attract his attention, waving my arms and pointing to outside the window and mimed by crossing my index fingers indicating, as best I could, the unmoving propeller outside.

At the same time I was smiling broadly as if there was nothing untoward. He was on an aisle seat and he nodded, but it was obvious he didn't know what I was referring to at all.

But he soon did, and my stupid explanation shattered.

The intercom clicked on. The Captain's (quite calm) voice…

'Ladies and Gentlemen. Your Captain speaking… We have some technical trouble. Nothing to be concerned about, but I have to tell you and apologise because we have to return to London. I will report further…'

So there. Of course they don't 'rest' engines like that. Stupid of me.

The moon was now on the other side of the plane, and soon we were back at Heathrow.

We all disembarked, and then sent into the restaurant for some refreshment on the house, while awaiting details of the delay.

The delay went on, and so we were then given the dinner which we should have been having in Ireland at that time while still awaiting details of the new take-off…

By that time some hours had passed, and we had news. But not what we expected.

Apologies, apologies the delay would be even longer and so we were to be taken to a hotel overnight! We would be called early in the morning to be returned to the Airport.

Luggage reclaimed, and into buses, assuming the hotel was somewhere on the airport. But it wasn't. We were taken a long way right out into Surrey somewhere. Nearer Gatwick than Heathrow. And so to bed.

A fitful sleep, expecting news of having to get up quickly.

But no. Early morning tea was brought, but no message still. At least nothing of a repaired aeroplane.

Just, 'have your breakfast when you're ready. No hurry'.

'No hurry' indeed!

We were already late to start rehearsals in New York.

I phoned Margaret. She was so pleased that I'd landed safely and in such good time…

'No dear, I'm not in New York, I'm in Surrey…'

'Surrey! Where's that?'

'SURREY, you know that place, near Sussex…'

A pause.

She now was concerned.

'What are you doing there, what happened?'

I told her. No worry, but we still did not know when we would take off again.

In fact we were told that we should relax and why not play a round of golf during the day! It was a posh hotel with a full-size golf course.

It indeed was a lovely day for golf. I didn't play, I just sat around in the beautiful grounds…

But we ought to have been in NYC.

Eventually at long last we were picked up to return to the airport and the flight was scheduled to leave at just 24 hours late.

It did. And it was a re-run of the evening before. Margaret and the boys had come to see us off, again! Not so care-free I believe.

I wasn't so keen to check the starboard wing this time.

We did get to Shannon ok and had the meal. Breathing a sigh of relief we got across the Atlantic.

Or so we thought. But aghast we hadn't. That engine played up again, and this time the Captain decided to land at Keplavik (Iceland)…

Again we disembarked. It was cold and miserable. By now we were getting very worried indeed about missing our rehearsals. The time was short anyway before we had to open.

Stanley Baker was getting very angry. He had taken it upon himself to throw his weight about, which he could do very well.

Not that it seemed it would do any good. PanAm staff were not obvious at this outpost. Many of our fellow passengers were then following Stanley taking up the cry for something to be done.

It was clear that our plane was truly grounded.

The Balletmaster, Massine, was also a passenger on this flight, and it was noticeable to see that each time we had run into trouble, he had changed his hat. Trying to change his luck we were told.

An official was eventually found with some news, but not very much. A PanAm flight from Paris to New York had a few empty seats on it and it was being diverted to help us.

But it wasn't broadcast as it only had about five empty seats to fill. It might have only been as few as three.

Whatever, a big problem.

Who were going to get those seats?

Stanley pitched in, over-selling how 'a big first night in New York was in jeopardy', with all his Welsh fervour.

And it worked. It was still some time before the plane from Paris arrived, and we were up and away once again. Hoping…

I noticed that Massine had also been successful in getting one of the few seats available. Changing his hat and his luck seemed to have worked. We left behind in Iceland the bulk of the passengers all, no doubt, screaming angry that they had been left stranded.

This was my initial long-distance flight, and considering all the problems and the fact that it had taken so long I had no opportunity to relax at all. I was too concerned.

However, over the years following, during many long flights, I enjoyed the complete other-worldliness of being entirely cut-off above the clouds and it became a unique experience provoking me to start "word-doodling" (I certainly couldn't call it poetry!). Taking the pressure off day to day earthbound problems seemed to release my grey matter to start playing with words… letting them fly in fact… Passing time took on a new, freer, more relaxed element. The unreality of it all. I enjoyed that.

Alas! Time to ponder
Terra most firma
This broken-winged
apologetic
Pegasus.

I particularly remember on one of those later journeys being provoked (for fun), on reflection of the packaged meal aboard, to scribble a piece:

The bird was above Anticosti –
35,000 feet above.
How strange!
Flying? No, curried –
35,000 feet above
the ocean.

Where did that bird once roam?
That could hardly raise a wing to fly.
Some Canadian battery?
Can it be that mother hen straining the egg
Foresaw what heights her offspring chicken
Might attain?
Above the weather at 35,000 feet –
curried!"

Well, I warned you, reader. It was only 'doodling'.

But I must return to my first haphazard trans-Atlantic flight in 1951. Eventually, at long last we did get landed safely at Idlewild, NY Airport.

Then, to experience my baptism of the United States of America.

But, the shock was to continue – the culture shock to begin.

I was convinced that I knew America. I'd seen all the movies and we spoke the same language…

Wrong!

Chapter Seven

The New World

I had seen so many American films in my youth, I was sure that I "knew" the USA. Indeed, I had never thought of it as a foreign country, I was so familiar with it. Or, so I thought.

Shock number one: I was wrong. I didn't know that country at all. As soon as I stepped off that aircraft on Long Island, I soon discovered that I was the foreigner.

First I was so surprised with the climate. A dry heat, continental. Geographically, it had never occurred to me that New York was as far south as Spain! At home in Sussex I always imagined that just somewhere 'over there, straight West' was New York City. So wrong. Straight West from Sussex aligns with way up in Canada, north of Newfoundland!

And then as I got my first sight of the colour of the buildings on the drive from the Airport (not to mention the spelling) they looked all Mediterranean burnt-sienna.

Surprise, surprise.

In no time at all, I realised that I was the odd one out.

After the first experience of the tunnel into Manhattan, we (Stanley Baker was with me) were driven to the hotel reserved for us. A special one, very old Colonial, chosen by the American Producer, Luther Greene, as being right for the British boys. How wrong he was!

Hwfa (Hugh) Pryse had a sister in NYC and so he was staying with her, and Don Harron had, we discovered, brought his family, from Toronto, with him and had taken an apartment downtown. We, Stanley with me, were housed in the small, select, Winslow Hotel.

But only for one night.

The Colonial style, regime, and colour-consciousness was anathema to us. Stanley declared he was not going to stay there, and I agreed. In the short time I was there, when meeting the staff I tried to make pleasant conversation as was my habit, but very quickly I was made aware that it was NOT the done thing.

We stayed there just the one night, and then moved into the Henry Hudson hotel, on the Westside (57th St). Much more "touristy" and easy-going and crowded and to our taste, thankfully.

Next morning, it was pancakes and maple-syrup breakfast. Gee! So good. They became my staple diet for many years after when either in the States or Canada.

Stanley wanted to go to a Chemist (sorry, no, a drug-store). He'd forgotten his toothbrush. So, we wandered into one of those shops typical of North America, went up to the counter and he asked for a toothbrush.

That in itself was different because the average local person would have just gone up to the appropriate rack, and chosen a brush and then off to the checkout to pay for it. No nonsense. Quick as a flash, all done. Hardly a word spoken, except the obligatory, 'Have a nice day'.

But this was different. The girl behind the counter stood perplexed.

She just looked at him. I thought she fancied him. He was a very handsome young man. Time seemed to stand still for a few moments, and then she walked away. She joined two other girls at the other end of the shop, spoke to them and then brought them back to where Stanley waited. She requested him to speak again.

He did.

The girls were absolutely delighted! It was remarkable.

The first girl apparently had been so entranced at the sound of his voice, that she had to get the others to listen to it!

They obviously found Stanley's Welsh tones so unusual and attractive.

It was another example, early on, that we indeed were 'foreigners'.

I soon recognised that my method of speaking – quite apart from the different accent – my English, used far too many words in my sentences. My speech was decorative, elaborate, apologetic even.

At first I was self-conscious about it. But once I had acknowledged that we were not the same, and didn't speak the same language, I settled down.

Another vivid memory lingers from the first visit to the Church in which we were going to perform.

We got to St James's at Madison and 71st to meet the Producer Luther Greene (he was the husband of the famous Australian actress, Judith Anderson who I had seen in London, give her Lady Macbeth at the Old Vic).

As usual we assessed the space, testing the acoustics. It was (probably still is) a large pseudo gothic edifice. We walked around getting the 'feel' of it. We were impressed by the large stone pillars. That is, we were, until we tapped them as we walked by, and discovered that they were just hollow shells. Not solid gothic at all.

So, the acoustics were not favourable.

But Producer, Luther Greene, had anticipated this and introduced us to the sound engineer whom he had hired, 'the best sound man in the USA'.

That is, until, as that "expert" turned to shake Stanley Baker by the hand, when I noticed that he had a hearing-aid hanging from his left ear! We just about saved ourselves from falling apart with laughter.

We played the first performance (October 16, 1951) with all that so-called expert sound equipment in place, but for only that one performance. The second night and from then on we switched it all off. We preferred to rely on all the experience we had gained from adapting to all the English churches we had visited. It was better.

We had all the excitement of a debut, an American premiere of a new play in New York City. The first-night never being over until the visit to the famous show-biz restaurant, Sardis', after the show, to mix with the "names" and apprehensively pass the time until the morning papers arrived with the reviews.

If they were good, it was congratulations all round and extended celebration, if not, it was time to creep out unobserved.

Blessings be, we didn't have to creep out.

A lasting memento of that opening coverage was the excellent Hirschfeld cartoon of the four of us in the play that took up almost half a page in the *New York Times*.

It cannot be said that we "opened on Broadway" as such, but the American premiere of a new Christopher Fry play, created a lot of interest. *The Lady's Not For Burning* had been a hit the season before, but this was something quite different.

Yards of column inches paid it the respect the special event warranted. It represented the Festival of Britain in New York theatre:

'Broadway first-nighters attended an opening last night in surroundings vastly different from the glitter of the theatrical district... Places in St James' oaken pews were occupied by persons frequently seen at Broadway openings' (Gordon Allison).

The New York critics found lots to write about. Even when they found it 'difficult', 'intellectually oblique', 'confusion', 'illusiveness of the poetry'; they found much to admire and congratulate.

'The concrete authority of the performance must be recognised as a considerable achievement. Michael Macowan directed with great skill. Thank the actors for speaking the English language with grace and clarity. They use Mr Fry's verse beautifully. Their performance has the force and humanity – tense, homely and devout...' (Brooks Atkinson, *New York Times*).

'It is not an easy work to appreciate. You must meet it more than halfway, but I think that is an effort worth making. The English cast and Director are properly concerned with the work's philosophical values. Of the actors, all of them are excellent' (Richard Watts Jnr, *New York Post*).

'Having seen and heard Leonard White, Stanley Baker and Hugh Pryse in their roles, they are to put it bluntly, superb. After I've said they are superb, after I've meant they are superb, what is there left to say? In fact almost everything about Christopher Fry's *A Sleep of Prisoners*...' (Robert Garland, *New York Journal American*).

'Christopher Fry's *A Sleep of Prisoners* is a tremendously exciting experience. Vividly staged, the play has violence, frequent majesty and a lingering echo of inspiration... The sudden and surprising appearances are devised in a brilliant fashion which gives the play all the irrational clarity of a tormented dream. The cast is splendid' (William Hawkins, *New York World Telegram*).

'The tales of... Man's inhumanity, war's hell, all our sins of power politics and passive cynicism, are put to the twirl of the poet's intricately patterned rhythms and allusions, and – let's face it – reduced there to a sonorous guessing game. Directed by Michael Macowan, the Messrs. White, Harron, Baker and Pryse do play this game to their very active utmost. They show a great doubtless laudable determination to lift it all out of bleak sorrow and Gregorian chant. You'll find that Mr Fry still has a God-given freedom of fine phrases.' (*Cue*)

Nearly two weeks later, Brooks Atkinson of the *New York Times* was provoked to write another very long review of the play. Inspired by the splendid cartoon by Al Hirschfield which had appeared in the Sunday edition of that paper.

It was a very analytical, educational piece.

'Enthralled by the vivid spectacle of a drama played in the chancel. The rites of a drama... seemed to him (Hirschfield) not only beautiful, but appropriate and natural. Mr Fry's verse play has not parted company with a fundamental tradition. It is also extremely well acted and directed... A company that knows how to speak verse.'

But, Atkinson summarises, alas, with: 'Mr Fry has struck a few literary postures. The old miracle plays that were close to the church hundreds of years ago were crude and naïve, but they were pithier...'

For me who subsequently lived with that play for several years (playing in it and directing the premiere in Canada and some revivals) I found Christopher's dramatic essay on Man's violence, (as was my own definition of it) following World War II, so rich and deeply involving. Indeed after all that time living with it I've been continually frustrated in that I do not believe we ever achieved playing it to perfection. The challenging intricate quartet was so demanding. But so wonderful, nevertheless.

It became a turning point in my career.

After the highlight of the New York opening, things settled down and I was able to explore the wonders of Manhattan. To come to terms with this New World City. Contrasted with London theatre-going the curtain-up here was quite late in the evening, and so Stanley Baker with me would find ourselves walking away from 71st Street around midnight after the performance.

First a regular call at a nearby hotel for a drink at the splendid up-market bar. A far cry from the pub in Kingly street (back-vestry) after the show in London.

In the Madison Avenue venue I have hazy memories of often finding a group of Middle-East men there, and who for some reason seemed to find us suspicious. Their jocularity, even after they had discovered that we were "only actors", always seemed to have an edge.

Sinister? Maybe.

Otherwise we had pleasurable encounters with some of the backers of our play. Notably a group of Reverend gentlemen (Francitas Film Foundation/Southern Methodist University) from "down South" who – for Methodists – certainly enjoyed their beverage. Also I was fascinated to discover that they fervently prayed for the opponents of their University football team to LOSE!

Very Christian.

Also, I met Richard Burton there. He of course, as a fellow Welshman of Stanley Baker, had come to see his friend. Richard's American Agent was with him and he took on Stanley to represent him afterwards, which started his successful film career.

There was also a very classy attractive hostess there, who seemed to like us British. Subsequently, on a Sunday rest-day she wanted to show me the countryside and took me for a drive to her home to meet her family and to have tea (a nod to the English). I was astounded to discover that the drive was several hundred miles, there and back on the same day, and that didn't seem to be anything out of the ordinary. A highway jaunt seemingly.

However, daily, after the show and some refreshment American style, the routine continued usually by walking Downtown in the early hours, never a thought of getting to bed right away. Experiencing the City that never sleeps.

Taking in some food en-route at a typical Automat.

I was fascinated by being able to select something to eat, at a machine with a large bank of drawers; put your money in a slot and open the selected drawer to reveal your meal! Magic, I thought then. There was also a large cafeteria-type counter loaded with food if one wanted to be more selective.

I remember the first instance we tried choosing from that galaxy of food. I wanted a fresh-fruit salad. What a selection! I indicated to the guy behind the counter what I wanted. I just pointed. I had become very wary of the "limey" give-away if I spoke. Quick as a flash I got my plate-full of luscious fruit in stunning "colors". And then I had to speak.

I wanted some cream with my fruit salad.

'Can I have some cream with it?'

Everything stopped!

The guy behind the counter froze. I tried again.

'I'd… I'd… like some cream with my fruit salad, please…'

Without any response, the guy walked away from me to the other end of the counter – I thought, 'here we go again,' it was such a long counter – towards one other guy, and raised his voice:

'This guy wants some cream with his fruit salad!'

A pause. Quite a long pause… The other guy thought about it, and then uttered:

'Well, give it to 'im… Some people eat different.'

It was obviously not the done thing! They were both puzzled. Another example of my stupid assumption. What I took for normal was certainly not so there.

I was learning quickly.

However, the month or so in NYC enabled me to change from the strangeness of my first impressions to being able to much enjoy this new world.

Being amid the skyscrapers, and the environment of the 24-hour non-stop days, was exciting and stimulating. And I'd thought that

London was busy! And as for "Seely Sussex", well, certainly another world altogether.

The subway trains, (more like versions of our London District line only dirtier, and covered in graffiti (although we soon caught up with that); the Empire State and RCA edifices including those magical lifts (sorry, *elevators*) that shot at such speed to the tops; the Radio-City Music Hall.

The impressive open-air skating rink (Rockefeller Center) in midtown, the Broadway theatres, Times Square and the big Stores. No shortages there. Rationing was still in place at home. From Macy's I was so pleased to be able to send food parcels to Margaret and the lads.

And the hospitality of New York City.

Especially I caught up with a young man who had been introduced to me by fellow actor, Norman Webb, back in London. He was a young student "doing Europe" and had seen our play in the West End, and now finding that we had arrived in New York, caught up with us. He was Walter Diehl. His parents lived on Park Avenue, and regally they made sure I had a good time.

Wonderful people. Visits to the Twenty-One Club were special.

It was the beginning of a very long friendship, through his subsequent marriage to Martha Washington – a name to be conjured with, a descendent and a very lovely lady, and then raising their family (Lorin, Martin, Toni and Gina). Many visits to their homes in Scarsdale and Hartsdale; and then, also, beyond Walter's so sad, too young death.

Martha and the family, with her new husband, Karl Forman, have remained closely, and happily, in touch, ever since.

Many moons later, after the Wall came down in Eastern Europe, Karl was able to visit the home of his forebears, and with Martha set up a second home, enabling them to spend time in both Prague (Klanovice) and Florida (Sarasota). They introduced Margaret and me to their Czech home and we spent a lovely visit enjoying the discovery of Prague. Among the highlights was seeing a theatre production in their National Theatre. It had the unlikely title of *Bastard*, but based on the Faust legend, it included music, physical theatre and drama, all elements splendid, first rate. It remains one of the most impressive visits to the Theatre that I have ever had.

Back in NYC during the time in the "fall" of 1951, I caught up with Norris Houghton, who had directed Michael Redgrave's *Macbeth* in London, in which I played my Malcolm. Norris walked me around Broadway to show me the sights. The impressive skyscrapers funnelled the winds through the Streets and Avenues and I was surprised at the amount of litter. An odd thing to have remembered. I was also surprised to note some token attempts at air-raid shelters. It seemed strange so far from the war that I'd left behind.

My mentioning these observations, surprised Norris and he would soon change the subject and have me seated in a first-rate bar or restaurant illustrating the opulence of this new world.

What meals!

Other notable hospitality came from Lucille Lortel who, subsequently, was one of the Sponsors of our production on tour. Lucille was a well-known wealthy ex-actress, whose husband, I gathered was very rich. He ran a private radio station as a hobby. While I was there he made a special trip to England just to buy a Rolls Royce car which he promptly had shipped back to America with him.

Lucille lived near the Park at the Sherry Netherland and frequented the Park Plaza. She also lived in Westport, Connecticut, where she ran the famous White Barn Theatre in the grounds of their house; a centre for productions of special interest and presenting talent that Lucille felt ought to be seen.

She made sure that the cast of *A Sleep of Prisoners* were entertained splendidly, as visitors to the White Barn Theatre, one week-end.

As well as that playhouse, Lucille's husband provided her with the Theatre de Lys – the largest of the off-Broadway theatres in NYK – to enable her to present short showcase runs of the talent she wished to support. She first introduced Brecht/Weill's *Threepenny Opera* and it ran and ran and ran.

So much for limited runs!

Lucille, remained friendly and kept in touch with me throughout the years that followed. Particularly many moons later when I was in the role of producer of TV Drama and commissioning new writing. I regularly visited her on my subsequent trips to New York. She was a much respected friend until her death.

All too soon our limited run of *A Sleep of Prisoners* in NYC was coming to an end, and we then knew that we were going on tour.

But, before that, I received a letter, quite unsolicited, which certainly made sure that I realised I was in a foreign clime. It read:

Dear Mr White,

We regret to inform you that Ford's Theatre, Baltimore, practices a policy of racial discrimination, as Negro patrons are seated in the last row of the second balcony only. In protest of this un-American policy the local branch of the NAACP has been maintaining a picket line for five years at the theatre.

A number of prominent playwrights, directors, actors, and even entire casts of plays have refused to play Ford's because of the segregation. The list includes, Charles Boyer, Madeline Carroll, Irvin Berlin, Lillian Hellman, Jean Pierre Amont, Jose Ferrer, Basil Rathbone, Jackie Cooper, Canada Lee, Todd Duncan, Lawrence Tibbett, Muriel Rahn, Olivia de Havilland, Uta Hagen, Ethel Waters, and Eli Wallach.

Member of the Wedding, St Joan, Romeo and Juliet, Rose Tattoo, were advertised for Baltimore by the Theatre Guild, but will not book here.

Although Baltimore is a "borderline" city, the old patterns of racial discrimination have changed greatly in the past several years. The Lyric, Olny, Hilltop (summer), Hopkins experimental theatres and auditoriums of the Baltimore Museum, Peabody Conservatory, Hopkins, Loyola, State Teachers and Notre Dame Colleges are open to all without segregation.

Negro students attend four of the above named institutions and the University of Maryland. There are Negro graduate nurses at Hopkins Hospital and one of the most exclusive hospitals here has opened to coloured patients. The City Dept of Recreation passed a ruling this summer admitting all citizens to golf courses, tennis courts, baseball and play lots. Interracial sport teams are welcomed also in

the municipal parks. Two weeks ago the Maryland State
Teachers Association voted to admit Negro teachers.
Mr Marcus Heiman, lessee of Ford's Theatre, has been
informed of these changes in Baltimore.

If members of the acting profession will take a firm
stand of disapproval in this case and refuse to play
Ford's as long as the house segregates, we believe
the theatre-going public of Baltimore will succeed
in convincing Mr Heiman that it is time to change his
policy here.

May we count on you to aid us in this struggle for
real democracy??

Sincerely yours,

(Mrs) Adah K Jenkins

Chairman

COMMITTEE FOR NON-SEGREGATION IN BALTIMORE THEATRES.

First on the tour we went to Washington DC. We played in the
Church of the Ascension and St Agnes. I stayed at the Burlington
Hotel.

Again, fortunately, there was time to savour, this capital city of the
White House (and white squirrels and black squirrels). The Washington,
Lincoln and Jefferson Memorials, the Supreme Court (with a barber's
shop just inside the main entrance!) and the Potomac River (displaying
numerous floating cast-off "rubbers"!). Contrasts indeed.

Trips into Virginia – the Arlington Cemetery. And for the first time
a taste of the South was evident.

On my visit to the Capitol I was tickled to discover on a plaque listing
the Pilgrim Fathers that arrived on the *Mayflower* in 1620 the names of
William White and his family. I just stood there and imagined that my
forbears might have been on that boat! Only dreamed of course...

As I've never known anything of my ancestry further back than my
paternal grandfather, it could only be wishful thinking.

We played there for two weeks.

Ernie Schrier of the *Washington Times-Herald* wrote two long reviews
of the play (Nov 20 and 25th 1951):

'Currently Washington is seeing Fry, not as a witty word-vendor, but as a crusader bent on restoring peace and harmony to humanity... We take to Fry because his particular kind of poetry is unique in the Theatre today. The language he uses hasn't been written in over 300 years...'

Mr Schrier didn't like it very much.

Jay Carmody (*Washington Evening Star*) wrote:

'It is greatly to the advantage of *A Sleep of Prisoners* that its poetry is read by actors unaffected by the mere shape of Fry's speech. It is thus given meaning as well as music... It is to their credit that Fry's allegorical acrobatics are so engrossing that the spectator quickly loses a feeling of strangeness at seeing a play in a church.'

Richard L Coe of the *Washington Post* (November 27, 1951), wrote a fine and probably the most sensible appraisal of this play. He didn't find it confusing as some did, or difficult.

'Fry is a quiet country-loving fellow who clearly has not stooped to mass appeal, a phenomenon in our money-conscious culture. That he chooses, as in this play, to assume that audiences have some knowledge of the Old Testament and give any thought to why violence constricts civilization is an approach wholly at variance with theatrical custom...

'On the matter of construction all this is ingeniously worked out. But it is not so difficult to follow as Fry's critics suggest. It is simply that his paths are unfamiliar, but by the end of the play he brings us to a clear statement...

'Fry's poetry, compared with the measured words of Eliot resembles a farmer who has just discovered his tongue. Every thought he has, pertinent or elliptical comes tumbling out of his mouth. The torrent of words, thoughts, allusions and humor... Yet it is the bubbling of a civilised mind and not the unabashed outpourings of a sentimental one as in the case of Saroyan, whose same disciplinary fault was treated as a virtue by his early admirers...

'But, clarity and hope are in this play...

'This is ensemble play-acting of the first order, a string quartet in human form. Those who are weary of the obvious and commercial will find much to absorb and challenge them in *A Sleep of Prisoners*.'

Next into Maryland to Baltimore (Congress Hotel). We played in Old St Paul's Church.

Thus, we did not offend the Committee for Non-Segregation by playing at Ford's Theatre. And I was glad to begin to taste the USA away from the unique experiences of Manhattan and DC.

After that in the State of Delaware, to Wilmington. Thence to Pennsylvania, and the Liberty Bell city of Philadelphia. There to ponder the extraordinary vision and endeavour of William Penn in setting up that Quaker State, and yet the man who found retreat in a small Sussex village – my home county.

In Philadelphia we played in St Paul's, Chestnut Hill.

I have warm social memories of being welcomed by Mr and Mrs (Cornelia) Dam. And, subsequently, months later, when visiting London, they hosted Margaret and me at the Caprice Restaurant (if you couldn't get in to the Ivy, you went to the Caprice).

The "notices" continued to be fine and stimulating. In Philadelphia's *Evening Bulletin*, Harrison W Fry (no relation to our Christopher) included this in his long review: 'If you expect moralizing, if you expect a clear-cut evangelistic appeal, if you expect saints dressed up in soldiers uniforms, you will not find them in Fry's play. You will find yourself – whether you have been a soldier or not – opening your mind to let the broad panorama of the universe and the questions it raises sweep in.'

The concept of Christopher's fine creation, so aptly put.

Henry T Murdock of the *Philadelphia Inquirer* ended his review with: 'The fullest of praise must be given the quartet who enact the drama… Playing little short of brilliant is given by Leonard White, Stanley Baker, Donald Harron and Hugh Pryse, while of equal merit is the direction of Michael MacOwan. They have joined Fry in creating a provocative, disturbing and memorable piece of theatre.'

Such made the work so worthwhile in what might have been otherwise an arduous tour.

Next a winter train journey en-route to Pittsburgh. An experience in itself. My previous short trips on the London Brighton & South Coast Railway line, as it was – becoming the Southern Railway – and occasionally the London & North-Eastern, hardly prepared me for a continental railroad. Exciting.

A silly memory, but it was the first time I'd been introduced to the special *Combination Ham and Cheese* sandwich, available on that train. Sandwiches I'd had before, of course, scores of them, and of the "proper" sort, notably *Oscar Wilde Cucumber*, daintily cut. But this was an American sandwich. And what a difference! Great!

Some people eat different.

It was a dark and very cold winter night when we arrived in Pittsburgh, and as was my habit upon arriving in any new town, going to the hotel and finding my room, I merely threw my bag on the bed, and then went out for a walk to acclimatise myself. This time it was different. Acclimatise is indeed the right word.

First, for a large busy city I was strangely aware that there were hardly any pedestrians about. And not very many cars!

But I continued walking. That is, I continued walking for only a short time before I became aware that I couldn't feel my nose! My *Mad Dogs and Englishmen* image hadn't realised that this temperature was cold, the like of which I'd never experienced. I immediately had thoughts of frostbite, and sharply made a move for the nearest coffee-shop. I stayed there long enough to get the blood circulating again and then braced myself to make a quick dash back to the hotel.

Hello Pittsburgh!

Two firsts here. We played in the Pennsylvania College for Women and we had a new member of the cast. Hugh Pryse who had been playing the character of Tim Meadows since the start, got himself cast in a new Allan Ladd film.

Quite apart from Hugh's excellent talent, he was just about the right size to appear with Allan Ladd.

Many moons later when I had finished the tour and I was back in New York I met up again with Hugh and he told me of that experience. He related how when in a two-handed scene with Allan Ladd even he had to be dug into the ground to give the star dominance! And Hugh was not very tall himself... very short in fact.

As for our cast change, a fine leading Anglo/American character actor joined us. Clarence Derwent. He had strong connections with English theatre, being born in London within the sound of Bow Bells and who as a schoolboy had been greatly impressed by Sir John Irving, and who became a member of the famous Sir Frank Benson's Shakespeare company: and indeed after his death to this day is responsible for the Clarence Derwent Award given to young actor talent in the UK.

He made his debut with us at Pittsburgh.

In his autobiography covering the first fifty years of his career (Henry Shuman Inc., NY, 1953), Clarence wrote 'I came to regard *A Sleep of Prisoners* as one of the finest plays in which I have taken part.'

Kaspar Monahan wrote in the *Pittsburgh Press*, "It was a unique experience last evening for the first-nighters who braved the icy hill roads... to see Mr Fry's allegorical dream play... a highly commendable project. Its tour through the nation promises to be a rare event unparalleled in theater history."

Only Stanley Baker and myself now remained of the original cast.

Then we were on our way to Michigan, the city of Detroit (St John's Episcopal Church) for eight performances.

An unusual way to spend Christmas. We actually opened on Christmas Day. We read the reviews on Boxing Day – except it wasn't Boxing Day there of course. Yet another example of expectation that things/customs would be the same there as we limeys were used to having. Wrong again. Celebrations there were all in the family homes. Our hotel seemed dead; was dead. Everyone had gone home.

Our tour manager promised us a party. Nothing materialised. Well, almost nothing. Just two or three of us on our own in one of our rooms with a very soberly drink.

Goodbye wintery Detroit.

On to Chicago. On the journey I was surprised when the train slowed down and I saw the station sign Kalamazoo! I thought that was only a fictitious name used in the song. I'd couldn't believe that it was a real placename. But, there it was, plain to see. Kalamazoo hello, goodbye.

And so, to Chicago, where we stayed longer, using that as base for some venues nearby. The windy city on the great lake Michigan; an impressive skyline.

The EL, the huge stockyards for corned beef, spearmint skyscraper, rows of burlesque theatres, great jazz clubs and prohibition ...and the *Daily Tribune*.

Not to mention the pro-Irish, anti-British atmos.

On January 16th 1952 the *Chicago Daily Tribune* published a cartoon by Orr which depicted a caricature (a Churchillian figure) dressed as John Bull wearing a Union Jack waistcoat, a Royal cloak and a crown; standing in a wintery London scene (Big Ben in the background), holding out a top hat containing a few pencils for sale with a notice board stuck in the ground declaring 'Begging since 1917'... It made me mad.

I wrote a letter to the editor of the *Tribune*. They printed it and gave it a heading – *An Englishman Protests*.

```
Chicago, Jan 16.

As an Englishman having the privilege to be
in the United States at the moment, I feel I
must congratulate your cartoonist, Orr, on his
interpretation of the present day "John Bull", with
"diamonds in his crown and pencils in his hat". It is
so obviously designed to make for better understanding
and friendship between our two peoples!

In my short time here it has become noticeable that
the attitude of the average Britisher is almost as
unknown to the average American as that to the average
person beyond the iron curtain. I therefore think
it would hardly be amiss if I pointed out that in my
experience no one in Britain wants further aid (in
a monetary sense) from the United States. In fact,
I think that people as a whole would rather deprive
themselves still further of their livelihood than
become still more "indebted" to the United States by
loan or suchlike. People over there value whatever
independence they have far too highly to give it up
lightly.

I do not presume to know what will be the outcome
of the visit here of our prime minister but I have
sufficient faith in Mr Churchill's ability as a
statesman of the world to know that the motives are
```

```
of the highest. From a nationalistic point of view
however, I feel personally that any further need for
aid from the United States would be viewed by the
people of Britain with great displeasure.

   It would indeed be better for us to have the answer
"No", than to be granted the requests and then later
to have the fact rammed down one's throat by such as
'Orr'.
```

But that of course is only one side of the story in Chicago. My overall impression was that I was in the first example of a truly American city.

Very different.

We played first in Temple Sholom, Lake Shore Drive – Christopher Fry having largely used the Old Testament stories it perhaps made the play appropriate.

We opened there on New Year's day, 1952. Many moons after that when I'd got back to London, I was told that *A Sleep of Prisoners* had been banned by the Anglican church in Australia because it 'did not deal with the New Testament'. (I believe that the ban was lifted later.)

Claudia Cassidy (*Chicago Daily Tribune*) in her review was able to compare this presentation in Temple Sholom with the original at St Thomas's in London and found it 'Less at home'.

'Playing its first performance in a synagog was not a matter of Jewish or High Anglican background that made it less at home than when I first saw it in the dingy, damaged, ancient and mysterious dusk of St Thomas' in London. It was a matter of architecture, of lighting, of intimacy. Of cast changes, of the receptive mood, which was then, in its quiet way, a matter of pilgrimage… Still, this is not a play I would want to miss, even in its present less satisfactory, condition…It has power to reach out, and touches of glory too.'

Temple Sholom, Chicago, also provided another first. Through the auspices of our new member of cast, Clarence Derwent, I was asked if I would join him in an invitation we had been made to talk about the play to the congregation on the Saturday.

I was indeed honoured to be asked, but after some very heavy thinking, I was just too scared – not sure enough of myself at all – to be able to do it. In the end, our Canadian, Donald Harron joined Clarence in doing so. Donald welcomed the impromptu audience.

In playing in the Temple I remember it for the fine audiences and being one of the best for acoustics that we encountered. Especially when compared with other venues in Chicago, such as the People's Church, which was not unlike an Albert Hall, where we were playing almost "in the round" to tiers upon tiers of auditorium. Not conducive to our intimate four-hander. Amazing that we got away with it at all. But somehow, thankfully, we did.

By then, Lucille Lortel, had taken over from Luther Greene as our Producer for the tour.

We also played in the University of Chicago, Rockefeller Chapel, the First Congregational Church, Oak Park and the First Methodist Church, in Evanston.

Quite a rich mix of congregations/audiences!

Indeed Evanston ('posh Evanston') was a considerable contrast.

There, through the auspices of the British trade ambassador in Chicago, I – sharing with Donald Harron – had the luxury of staying in a full-blown apartment on Diversey Parkway. And experienced hospitality galore in private parties; the highlight of one, hosted splendidly by Mr & Mrs Daggett Harvey and their daughter Jean at which I met Edward G Robinson. A great surprise. And to find him a quiet sensitive man so unlike his film persona. He was playing the lead in the powerful adaptation by Sidney Kingsley, of Arthur Koestler's novel *Darkness at Noon* at the Erlanger Theatre. I was very glad to have seen it there..

Also at that time at the Erlanger I saw Olivia de Havilland play the lead in Shaw's *Candida*. (Catching up on the work of Norris Houghton who directed it). Elsewhere I saw *South Pacific* with Janet Blair/Webb Tilton (Shubert Theatre) and supported our Sadler's Wells Theatre Ballet (lead by David Blair and Svetlana Beriosova) on their visit to the Opera House. And a concert by the Chicago Symphony Orchestra, of which Rafael Kubelik was in charge.

As a complete contrast I was introduced to the night-life at a local club to hear some great jazz.

There, prohibition gave all this the air of everything under wraps, behind closed doors. The entrance to this small club was a nondescript locked door, only big enough to let one person through at a time. Inside, blackness, only pierced by pinlights over cash-desks and the musicians in spotlights. Full of people. Full of noise. Very noisy. But good Jazz.

Applause and appreciation of a good time. The drinks flowed.

During our stay there, Lucille Lortel, our new Producer, set up a special dinner for us, her cast, in the Marine room at the Edgewater Beach Hotel (January 12, 1952). I wish I'd saved the menu! But I do have the photograph. Guests at our table were Lucille's sister, Ruth Cugat (married to the famous band-leader, Xavier Cugat) and Ellen Baker (Stanley's lovely wife visiting him, and who, of course later became Lady Baker). One of those special occasions when I so wished that Margaret could have been there.

Xavier and his big band entertained us... All exhibiting flamboyant and essentially white American luxury.

This city of contrasts and culture was also being demonstrated by our (Stanley and me) exploring the string of Burlesque theatres cheek by jowl (literally!) one after the other, which existed down main street. A new experience indeed. Starting at one end with some of them exhibiting (it might be said) respectability and dwindling the further one went down the street, into non-stop 24-hour strip shows.

My only lingering memory is that I had enormous sympathy for the routine obligatory comedians who often would be performing (non-stop) to nearly empty houses, and with those very few customers, asleep!

Contrasts indeed!

Neither the posh Edgewater Beach Hotel or Minsky's "Fountain of Youth" Burlesque theatre were ideally suited to the lifestyle of us performing Christopher Fry's war-stricken soldiers.

But the unique extended stay in Chicago soon transformed and we were back into our own reality. The play's the thing.

We continued to get audiences of great appreciation and reviews a pleasure to read. (Thank you Christopher).

One such write-up I just have to copy here. Headed *A Lawyer on the Aisle* and written by Philip R Davis, in the *Chicago Daily Law Bulletin* it projected an unusual view.

'Christopher Fry's poetic story is acted out with such fervid fidelity by four Englishmen (actually three English and one Canadian) as to make necessary a program note "You May Applaud", for the audience is left stunned and spellbound.

'While the beautiful Temple Sholom does not lend itself as well to the play's background of a bombed out church used temporarily as a prisoner-of-war camp as did St Thomas' in London. The lighting and stage setting coupled with the four prisoners, the tortured trapped men who seek release in their dreams make up for the inadequate background.

'Leonard White, as Private David King, tells his story with a magnetic abandon and poetic intensity. Stanley Baker as Corporal Adams has firmness and stolidity in his awareness of the poetic demands and physical requirements. while Donald Harron, as the weakest of the four trapped prisoners, is an intense if disingenuous private. Derwent (who happens to be President of Actors' Equity) is pleasing as he plays God with humour in the dream sequences, and Private Tim Meadows as an aging infantryman.

'There is a terrific fight between Stanley Baker and Donald Harron that will make you sit on the edge of your seat and with the same almost unbearable intensity the poetic words are hurled as the conflict between good and evil error and hope reach out of the troubled wings of time to bring a message more than entertainment to you and me.

'These expert actors have done a better job of speaking poetry than I have ever seen. You will be well rewarded for your pilgrimage to Temple Sholom at 3520 Lake Shore dr., for this is a play for a church as well as a theatre.'

So we soldiered on...

Into a different tempo with one and two-night stands.

By train to Madison, Wisconsin into the frozen Lake Mendota and finger-lakes country, and for the first time to present our production in a theatre, the University of Wisconsin Union Theatre. After that performance there the students gave us a rousing send-off, overnight onwards in our own coach, attached to an incoming train en-route to Toledo, Ohio. There it was a one-night performance back in a church, and briefly I was at the Willard Hotel. No time to "do" the town.

Next day to Cleveland and now to test the performance in a usually commercial theatre – the Hanna. Testing it was. A one-act play with a small fit-up set and just four actors and hardly Noël Coward or Tennessee Williams, in a large theatre, was asking a lot of that audience. And a lot of us!

It was warmly rewarding in that it found such a good response under such unfavourable circumstances.

William F McDermont (*Cleveland Plain Dealer*) wrote: 'It is mystic and often obscure both in its symbolism and in its language. But it has a kind of curious power and beauty…Fry has exceptional qualities both as a poet and a dramatist. He will write some murky and cryptic lines and then he will strike you with a stab of imagery so right and true and beautiful that it could emanate only from a genuine poet…It is beautifully played. Four characters are sharply differentiated and the actors materialise these differences with a stirring skill and vividness… an honorable enterprise'.

Omar Ranney of the *Cleveland Press* pointed out 'mixed reactions' in this surprising setting, and only to be expected but, he did write: 'However, those who are game for some mental exertion will, I believe, find this well worth the effort. The performances by the cast are all Grade A.'

But quickly on to Youngstown, Ohio. I don't have memories of Youngstown.

One-night stands such as this (February 4, 1952) don't lend themselves to detail, especially over fifty years later. But my scrapbook does confirm our presence in that town with one photo from the *Youngstown Vindicator*, a rather a good still showing me in my King David dream after Joab has killed his son, Absalom. And one member of St John's church there did wrote a congratulatory letter to Producer Luther Greene, to which I refer later.

That's as far West in the States as our tour took us.

Next a long journey back east into New York State to Rochester on the US side of Lake Ontario. Our Canadian Donald Harron got very frustrated in us not crossing the lake and the border into Toronto to show his family how well he was doing.

Rochester, home of Kodak, and again we were playing in a theatre – a big one – The Auditorium Theatre. But in spite of all our worries again about presenting our intimate play in such a big space theatre, we were so thankful to find that it had worked well there. In fact, according to critic AJ Warner of the *Rochester Times-Union* (February 6, 1952), it had worked very well.

'It is not easy even to attempt to convey something of the great and mystical spirit of Christopher Fry's *A Sleep of Prisoners*, which came to the Auditorium Theatre last night... Knowing that it was intended to be performed in church, I was disappointed that Rochester was not to see it in an ecclesiastical setting. But no sooner had the curtain gone up last night that I forgot everything save the ineffable poignancy and imagination which make this work memorable... Certainly, in the opinion of this reviewer, last night's performance was profoundly moving and beautiful with remarkable clarity and intelligibility... Fry's lines are of the essence of poetic lyricism, not really obscure, if he that has ears will let himself hear. A perfect cast, each of the four players speaking Fry's lines with distinction and eloquence, and acting their respective roles superbly.'

We played there for three nights to give us a little respite from the one-night stands and the long journey. That spread resulted in small audiences in that big 'house'. And AJ Warner ended his review with: 'That Rochester so little appreciates the high literary and dramatic privilege of seeing and hearing so remarkably fine a performance of Christopher Fry's striking play, as to turn out in pitiful small numbers, is a sad commentary on our local culture.'

Recharged with such appreciation, we were soon on the railroad again, via the Lehigh Valley.

But before that, while we were in Rochester we got the news of King George VI's death, and not unnaturally, two of us, Stanley and me, made the headlines in the *Rochester Times-Union*, February 6th, 1952:

'British-Born Residents Sad, Hopeful.'

And we were quoted: 'Two visitors to this country Leonard White and Stanley Baker pointed out that though they have been prepared for the king's death for some time "it really comes as a great shock". Said Baker: "The British people have felt great respect for him because he has carried on his job against his illness. Elizabeth too commands great respect for a girl of her age. I feel she is going to be an important link with this country and Canada. She was so well received on her visit here." White pointed out that George had endeared himself to his people for the heavy work he carried on although he was never in good health. But I have always held a private feeling that we had so magnificent and glorious a reign under our other Queen Elizabeth that we may have it again under this one.'

Now for a complete change of venue, to Cornell University at Ithaca, New York.

The move back eastwards had a hidden motive insofar that our Producer. Lucille Lortel – we learned later – wanted the production to have another run in NYC. As it turned out for many reasons, mainly contractual, that wasn't possible.

But onwards. Now at the campus at Cornell, a wintery scene but a students' warm welcome.

Quickly after that, to the home of the chocolate bar – the Hershey. Hershey, Pennsylvania. We stayed at the Community Inn on the corner of Chocolate and Cocoa Avenues. So Fry's comes to Hershey's!

Forgive me. I think I've warned of my bad jokes.

Allentown, also in Pennsylvania, after that, was really something different. Incredibly so. We played in the Lyric Theatre there. A small "house" and so no worries about size at this venue. But, a great surprise awaited us when we looked at the bills outside advertising forthcoming shows, to find *A Sleep of Prisoners* following a week of strip-tease burlesque! Girlie pictures alongside our sober-serious offering.

Sadly, I have no reviews of that date. Probably there were none. Surely confusing for the audience of that theatre which certainly had such a varied programme of "culture"! I believe we were followed by a recital given by President Truman's singing daughter.

Clearly all were catered for…

We were now on a run-down to the end of our tour, jumping about from Pennsylvania, to New Jersey and then to Connecticut…

Two University showings were at Princeton, NJ and at New Brunswick, NJ. In New Brunswick it was at Rutgers, an all-female college.

Clarence Derwent in his biog, highlights two of the University audiences: 'Countless came round after each performance declaring it to be the greatest experience they had ever known in the theatre. At Cornell and Princeton the standees were jamming the aisles over an hour before the performance began.'

Then, ending in Bridgeport (Conn) with a two day stay, including a matinee which was unusual, playing in the United Church there. And so, in a way, as we began, ten months before at Oxford.

The last review (by Fred Russell, *Bridgeport Post*, February 16, 1952) headed it as a 'passing show'. He, unlike earlier reviewers, found it difficult to imagine it being performed elsewhere other than a church: 'The church setting provides the atmosphere needed to get the most out of this poetic drama'.

He went on: 'The important thing is that it is done in Fry's wonderful gift for using words. After listening for a few minutes of his golden dialogue you are ready to forgive him for trying to get a message across just as long as he keeps the magic lines flowing... a cast that effectively and pleasantly brings to life the engaging symphony of the playwright's lines and has the audience clinging to every word... White is outstanding... all handle the Fry lines to perfection.'

Thanks for that epilogue.

We went our separate ways.

Afterwards I stayed in New York for a little while taking in the theatre. The Oliviers had arrived with their double-bill, the Shaw and the Shakespeare *Anthony and Cleo* and *Caesar and Cleo*, and it was good to see several old pals were in the casts. Notably Donald Pleasence who was staying in the same hotel as me – the Hotel Henry Hudson. Strange to find such an inexpensive hostelry almost opposite the very expensive Astor. That is, it was surprising until I discovered upon returning to the hotel one day, a notice on the front door from the Police declaring it a 'raided premises'... I then knew. The room walls were so flimsy and the noises beyond were obvious to say the least!

Saving hard-earned dollars, I remained there for the short time. It was conveniently in the heart of Broadway and even in that environment it was possible to eat cheaply.

I remember visiting Donald soon after arriving back in NYC and was impressed by his New World ingenuity when he invited me to have a meal in his room, and it turned out he had no cooking facilities but proceeded to demonstrate that he could boil an egg without even a saucepan or stove. He had bought a wonderful electric gizmo rather like a pencil, which he merely put into a tumbler glass, filled it with water dropped in the egg, and plugged the tiny heater into the electric socket, and hey presto in the prescribed time, he served me my boiled egg for tea…The wonders of the New World.

During this return to NYC, my short visit was enhanced by being able to see – apart from the Oliviers – Rex Harrison and Lilli Palmer in Christopher Fry's *Venus Observed* (New Century Theatre); Uta Hagen in Margaret Webster's production of Shaw's *St. Joan* (with Andrew Cruickshank and John Buckmaster at the Cort Theatre); Phil Silvers in a new Musical, *Top Banana* (at the Winter Garden Theatre); Jose Ferrer and Judith Evelyn in Joseph Kramm's *The Shrike* (Cort Theatre); and James Barton with Olga San Juan in *Paint Your Wagon* (another new musical of that time at the Shubert Theatre).

All representing the vibrant theatre in that city.

As we had finished our tour of *A Sleep of Prisoners*, a letter was received from Luther Greene, our original American Producer, in which he wrote: 'I have had many letters from where you have played praising you for your performances and your deportment. I quote from one which is typical:

'I was delighted with the very fine way in which the actors, stage hands, stage manager, and all the rest of your staff conducted themselves, They have a genuine concern to give a first class performance, and they did. It was a great thing for the city of Youngstown to be able to have the show here and I am deeply appreciative of your willingness to bring it for a one night stand (John H Burt, *St Johns Youngstown Ohio*).'

On February 17th, 1952, I was invited to the Memorial Service for King George VI being held in Church of the Transfiguration (known as the "Little Church Around the Corner") on East 29th Street. 'Particularly for the English players in America.' The lessons were read by Richard Greene (it was meant to be Basil Rathbone) and Brian Aherne, and the Address given by Sir Laurence Olivier – our local Baron of Brighton.

We had started our American adventure in a Church on Madison and 71st and ended it in another Church on East 29th NYC. For quite different reasons.

A lot had gone on between – thankfully, successfully.

As a matter of fact, I very nearly stayed on in NYC. Surprisingly, an Agent, Francis Head, who had been following our tour, and helping us, got me cast in a lead role in a TV play coming up. I was torn! She had gone to considerable trouble I know to get me considered and then cast, but I turned it down. I was by this time very homesick, and I'd got my passage booked, I just couldn't face being away any longer.

Francis Head wasn't pleased… Rightly so.

So, with Stanley Baker, on March 7th, 1952 we made our way to Hoboken Docks to embark on the SS Ryndam (Holland-America Line) for Southampton.

Fellow actor, Hugh Pryse, who was staying on in NYK for a while, saw us off, as did actress/anglophile Dorothy James (wife of one of our Producer's staff on the tour). Dorothy kept up her friendship for many moons, and we worked together briefly later.

It was good to sail the Atlantic and relax.

I remembered the hazardous outward journey by plane…

'Time to ponder, that broken-winged Pegasus.'

The weather was good. I settled down to read the passenger list. I noted we only had the Tourist Class names. Mustn't mix with First of course. I scanned the almost 480 names. There was none I recognised. Except, of course, 'Mr. Stanley Baker' who, like me, was eager to get back home.

Stanley's lovely young wife, actress Ellen, and my Margaret would occasionally meet in Hounslow High Street at week-ends when both would be shopping and visiting family.

But then, for me, it was being content to enjoy the week riding the Atlantic on SS Ryndam. Reflection and anticipation. My little Kodak camera had done overtime, snapping away at anything and nothing.

How photography has changed. Those prints then were so small, needing a magnifying glass to really see what was on them. I can just about see that at one time we passed the Cunarder, *Queen Elizabeth*, en-route back to New York.

And I taxed my memory trying to make sure I knew just where I had taken all the photos during the tour. More for all the albums at home. And there they remained. Clutter.

In my deck chair, I browsed among the papers I'd collected. Difficult to throw away. I studied the letters. More clutter?

Many moons later, looking at them after some fifty-five years, there's a shock or two. I'd forgotten that the tour hadn't been all plain-sailing…

I'd forgotten that I'd been Equity Deputy for the tour and that we'd had some contract problems. I do remember that we had little time to get contracts organised before we left London. I was reminded that I hadn't been happy myself about going at all when I knew that Denholm Elliott wasn't available to go with us. I didn't want to break up the team. It took some time to persuade me to go. Then we noticed that the contract was covering the 'run of the play', which we considered was for the premiere run in New York. It was only at the last moment we discovered that unlike a UK contract, this term 'run of the play' meant in the USA to cover any touring to follow.

We were not happy about that and wanted separate terms for any touring, and immediately alerted the American producers. Time was critically short, but we got a verbal assurance that Luther Greene (Producer) would discuss the touring element when got to New York. That was not satisfactory but we agreed. Alas, when we got to New York and opened, Mr Luther Greene declared that he knew nothing about it and insisted that we honour the contract as it was for the 'run of the play', no matter what. As Equity Deputy, I put the matter in the hands of American Equity.

Unfortunately the American Union did nothing to help us. The British Equity interpretation of 'run of the play' was not theirs. They declared that the Producer was right, we had signed in effect to include the tour. Alas!

One of the many examples to remind me that we were then in a "foreign" country. Stupid of me to assume that the English language meant the same thing in the USA as in the UK. Naïve in fact.

Happily, however, those old letters also revealed fortunately how successful it had all been.

In particular, one from a John R Tuerk of *The News in New York*:

Dear Mr White,

This is something I do not habitually do, but I was so moved and impressed after seeing your play, that I felt a letter to each of the cast members of "A Sleep of Prisoners" was necessary.

Not that my opinion is worth much, being just a member of this newspaper's staff. I still wanted you to know how much I had enjoyed your performance as Private David King. You made the character, at all times, alive and vibrant, both in reality and the dream sequences. Everyone of the adjectives that an actor works for could apply to your performance. Congratulations!

Thank you, for your part in affording the entire audience with such an enjoyable and thrilling evening.

Good luck during your run in New York. I hope to revisit your play before you conclude your engagement – that's how highly I thought of it.

Sincerely, John R. Tuerk.

That was pretty special.

Another was from the Chairman of the Theatre Club in NYC (Arline Williams) who wrote: 'I thoroughly was at one with your splendid performances,' and she invited me to attend her members at the Hotel Astor for tea and to speak 'about the play which would surely stimulate intelligent interest in your remarkable production'. I was very glad to accept her invitation. A rare occasion for me.

Thomas J Smith Jnr. wrote from Galveston, Texas, after only reading about the play – 'this new venture in the theatrical world. To perform a play in church and charge admission I'm sure startled many people, but having read what the play is about I can understand how fitting it can be for the sanctuary.'

And he asked for autographs of the cast 'for his collection'.

Daniel Blum, the Editor of *Theatre World* (NYC) wrote asking for 'records of my theatrical career' to be published in their Volume Eight yearbook.

Thus I presumed I was getting into the American theatre history. But I've never seen that publication, and so I have no confirmation. Probably, as usual, I was not included.

But the best memento was the truly lovely studio photograph that Margaret had got specially taken for me of her and the boys Martin and Stephen. To be with me during those long months away. A treasure it was. Later Margaret told me that Stephen was not at all cooperative in having his photo taken and that they had to make two visits to the photographer's studio to succeed.

Meanwhile the *Ryndam* made her way eastwards across the Atlantic, and news of my coming home was ahead of me (as I discovered later). On the day that I'd left Hoboken dock, the *North London Observer* (March 7, 1952) on its Feature Page ran a headline, 'Leonard White heads for Finsbury Park from the States'.

'His wife and family are looking forward to a reunion in Wilberforce Road...' Gee! Such excitement. But it was indeed such a lovely anticipation.

The voyage almost over. March 14th was the farewell dinner – Tourist Class. Six years after the war, *Tournedos Blanchette* was exotic.

And soon into sight of The Needles and Southampton Water. And soon back on the Southern Railway train due for Waterloo...

From the New World back to the Old, and in some ways very old. I was disappointed in that the train and the compartment that I was in was so grubby. Not a good greeting for those visitors from abroad, perhaps seeing England for the first time.

But, glory be! The grass was beautifully green, and the countryside lovely and comforting. And then eventually, Finsbury Park was looking good too, with the daffs blooming and lots of youngsters playing. But, that was over 50 years ago, when there was no fear in letting the children play on their own in the park.

And the few rooms we had at the top of 29 Wilberforce Road was very happily, with Margaret, and the boys, Martin and Stephen, "home sweet home" again.

So good to be back.

***

So far as my career, was concerned, I didn't know then this new year, 1952, was to be a watershed. I was shocked to find it was not easy to move on after *A Sleep of Prisoners*.

Even after many months of living with that play, acting that complex character of David King, it still remained unfinished business. I felt that we had never really achieved the challenge of that complete work. Occasionally we'd come close to it, but never the fulfilment.

It was indeed, difficult to follow.

What then?

What was going to provide the stimulating challenge, to be good enough, to be worthwhile? The prospect of "bread and butter" roles (pun NOT intended) was a puny prospect, not to be considered.

I didn't know it at the time, but things had to change.

But, as had been so much of the pattern before, my future turned out to be quite unplanned. Lap of the gods…

Anticipation was all…

Certainly not what I'd expected.

1953 here I come! TV highlights and *The Avengers* were not even in prospect…

As I close this, in early January, Margaret has just told me that the first daffodils are in flower in the garden. So early, so welcome.

'If Winter comes can Spring be far behind?'

Index

Coming Soon

Inside Story   *Out of this World*
Police Surgeon
Armchair Theatre (over 170 productions and an EMMY Award)
The Avengers (original Producer, first 40 episodes)
Playhouse   *Premiere*
Arrow to the Heart   *The Cat that Walked by Himself*
The Firstborn   *The Three Hermits*
After the Verdict   *Meeching Story*

***

Canada adventures
(Toronto, Edmonton, Regina, Ottawa, Banff)
CBC-TV

The Lady's Not for Burning   *The Metronome*
The Blood is Strong   *Relative Values*
A Sleep of Prisoners   *The Large Rope*
River Beat

***

Oxford Playhouse   Perth   Guildford
Hornchurch   Leatherhead   Coventry
Watford   Worthing Reps.

***

TWW TV   Tyne-Tees TV   Southern TV
HTV   Scottish TV   BBC TV

***

The Pretenders   *Bristol 600*
Item & M+M   *Seasons Greetings*
Sky   *The Georgian House*
Westway   *Crocodiles in Cream*
King of the Castle   *The Clifton House Mystery*
Our Little Town   *Murder at the Wedding*
Escape to the West   *Skin Deep*
Two Per Cent   *Preview*
Bookie   *The Old Master*
Stookie   *The Campbells*
Shadow of the Stone   *Strathblair*

Over 350 Drama productions for the UK Networks.

Many Moons
and a few more stars

in preparation